Renzo Chiarelli

Verona

new practical guide

*215 colour pictures
detailed map of the town
useful information*

BONECHI EDIZIONI "IL TURISMO"

Exclusive distributor for Verona:
Randazzo G. S.n.c. di Randazzo E. & R.
Via Emilei, 22 - 37121 VERONA
Tel. +39-45-800.40.40
Fax +39-45-803.60.63

Reprint 2002

© Copyright 2000 by Bonechi Edizioni "Il Turismo" S.r.l.
Via dei Rustici, 5 - 50122 FIRENZE
Tel. +39-55-239.82.24
Fax.+39-55-21.63.66
e-mail: bbonechi@dada.it
        info@bonechionline.com
http://www.bonechionline.com
Printed in Italy

Photos: Bonechi archives and Nicola Grifoni
Photos: page 34 (below) - kindly authorised by the Ministero per i Beni
Culturali ed Ambientali "Soprintendenza SBAS del Veneto".
Lay-out and cover: Lorenzo Cerrina
Photolitography: Fotolito Immagine, Firenze
Stampa: BO.BA.DO.MA., Firenze
ISBN 88-7204-337-9

Bird's eye view of the city.

VERONA "GATEWAY TO ITALY"

Verona, *Urbs Nobilissima*, is one of the most beautiful and ancient of all Italian cities - one which is justly famous and beloved both in Italy itself, and indeed, throughout the whole world. Today Verona has about 270 thousand inhabitants, and in the whole district of Veneto it is second only to Venice in wealth and importance.

Its climate and accessibility are ideal, and Verona is a vital rail and road junction on the main route connecting Italy to Central Europe. It is a flourishing industrial, commercial and agricultural centre of international importance and is the site of the annual *International Agricultural Show* and the *International Exhibition of Agricultural Machinery* - just two of the city's large exhibitions which attract visitors from all over Europe. The city is important in other fields as well - it is the home of the Mondadori firm of publishers, famous the world over. While on the subject of commerce, mention must be made of its wines, fruit, and of its marble, all of which are exported to many countries. Because of its fortunate geographi-

View of the city from the Roman Theatre.

cal position and its importance as a European city, Verona has been described as *The Gateway to Italy*. To travellers approaching from the North there is another sense in which Verona can be thought of as the *Gateway to Italy*. It is the first city which clearly possesses the appearance, harmony, character, the tradition and beauty of Italy, giving, as it were, a foretaste of the fundamental characteristics of the country as a whole. Verona's undeniable beauty has been celebrated by many foreign visitors who, from the earliest times have continued to pay tribute to the town in poetry and prose. Its beauty is essentially two-fold. Firstly, it is rich in natural beauty with its river, its hills, the nearby Lake Garda, and its background of mountains. Secondly, there is the great architectural beauty of the city itself with its buildings

and monuments. Verona is also an important cultural centre. It is a university city, with faculties of Economics, Languages, Education and Medicine, and a city rich in museums and distinguished libraries. But it is not just as an academic city that Verona has found fame, it has also become one of the major tourist centres of Italy. This is not surprising since the city as a whole is outstanding in what it has to offer the tourist. The people of Verona are friendly and welcoming, and a great deal of trouble is taken to make sure that the visitor really enjoys his stay. There are for example, theatrical performances staged during the warmer months, which include *operas in the Roman Arena* and *Shakespearean plays* staged in the Roman Theatre. There are Concert and Drama Societies and a highly

Piazza Bra.

renowned Academy of Music (Conservatorio di Musica). Finally we come to the one tourist attraction which makes Verona absolutely unique - its reputation thanks to Shakespeare and his play, as being the *town of Romeo and Juliet*.

This, then, is the city which we have set out briefly to describe, with its traditions, its fine buildings, its distinguished monuments.

NOTES ON THE HISTORY AND ART OF VERONA

The origins of Verona are lost in the mists of time; it is not even known how the city came by its name. All that can be said with certainty is that it was in prehistoric times that human beings first settled in the place where the city was later to rise. The date of the first Roman occupation is not known for sure, but by the 1st cent. B.C. Verona was already an important Roman settlement and the ancient centre of the town preserves the outlines of the original Roman nucleus which was known as *Augusta Verona*. Most of the important Roman remains in the town date from the 1st cent. B.C. The town centre, like all towns founded on Roman military camps is divided by the "cardus" and the "decumanus" - at right angles to each other - into four "quarters". In the number and quality of its Roman remains - the Amphitheatre, the Theatre, the arches, gates, and bridges etc. - Verona is second only to Rome itself. From very early days Verona's geographical position was a vital factor in the city's importance. Three of the most important Roman roads started from there - the Augusta, the Gallica, and the Postumia. The city's importance as a strategic centre, which was to last nearly a thousand years, became evident as early as the Late Empire. During this period, several decisive battles were fought in the neighbourhood of Verona, such as the battles of Claudius against the Germans in 368 A.D., Constantine against Maxentius in 312 A.D., and Stilicho against Alaric in 402 A.D. Even as early as the Roman period, Verona had already become a cultural centre and produced one of the greatest Latin poets: Q. Valerius Catullus.

S. Giorgio in Braida seen from the Roman Theatre.

In the Middle Ages, Verona was again the scene of important events. Theodoric stayed there, as did Alboin, the Longobard, who was murdered in Verona by his wife Rosamund. Later, Pepin, the son of Charlemagne, visited Verona as did Berengarius, the latter dying there in 924 in tragic circumstances.

Emperor Otto I of Germany came to the city to rescue Adelaide of Burgundy, who was held prisoner in the area. Despite invasions and wars, however, Verona still remained loyal to its cultural heritage. The city was fortunate in coming under the influence of two noble churchmen - the great Bishop St. Zeno during the 4th cent. and the kindly Archdeacon Pacifico in the 9th cent. Under the latter, there flourished one of the

Excavations have brought to light the Roman foundations of the Lion Gate.

most famous Academies of the period, the *Schola Sacerdotum*. The city developed its own distinctive style of art, and this, combined with the influence of the Carolingian and Ottonian style, enriched the city with Early Christian basilicas and Pre-Romanesque churches. At about this time also, the *Palace of Theodoric* was beginning to take shape on the banks of the River Adige.

During the troubled times of the early 12th cent., the Commune of Verona was formed. The city became deeply involved in the bitter wars which swept through the whole country. The greatest of these involved the conflicts between the Papacy and the Empire. In addition there were many purely local wars between

neighbouring cities. But in spite of these conflicts, Verona flourished, not only in trade, but also in the arts, and as a political centre. In 1164, under this first Council, the *Alliance of Verona* came into being. This united all the mainland cities of the Veneto against Barbarossa and was to lead to the subsequent League of Lombardy. In 1226, Verona became a possession of the tyrannical Ezzelino da Romano. Then in 1263, Leonardino della Scala nicknamed Mastino, was voted lord of the city, and thus began the rule of the great Scala (or Scaliger) family. Mastino was succeeded by Alberto, who died in 1301, and after him came his sons Bartolomeo, Alboino and Can Francesco. In 1308, Can Francesco became lord of the city, under the name Cangrande I. During his

Panorama from the Roman Theatre.
Facing page: ***St. Martin, high relief in tufa (Museum of Castelvecchio).***

rule, the dominance of the Scala family reached its most glorious height, with the city extending its influence over nearly all mainland Veneto. Cangrande, using his powers as the ruler of Verona, made the city into an antipapal stronghold. Its court became a cultural refuge and artists and writers flocked there in great number. Dante himself, who had previously been the guest of Cangrande's brother Bartolomeo, dedicated the third section of the Divine Comedy to his friend and patron, Cangrande. The death of Cangrande in 1329 marked the beginning of Verona's decline, despite the influence of a succession of distinguished rulers. One of them was Mastino II, under whose rule the sway of the Scala family was extended to include Brescia, Parma and Lucca. There was also Cangrande II, who built Castelvecchio and the superb bridge next to it, and then came the ferocious Cansignorio. The other great Italian ruling families, particularly those of Venice and Florence, often formed alliances against the Scalas, as did the Papacy itself. The rule of the Scala family finally came to an end with the flight of Antonio della Scala in 1387, after which the city fell into the hands of Gian Galeazzo Visconti. In 1404, Verona was conquered by the Carraresi, a powerful family from Padua; in 1405 it became part of the Venetian state. Venice retained its control over the city for nearly four hundred years, except for a brief period from 1509 to 1517, when Maximilian of Austria conquered it. Although the Venetian influence gave the city-state of Verona a long period of relative peace and prosperity, any suggestion of independence or desire for autonomy was firmly suppressed. As a result, the spirit and atmosphere of the city suffered severely. Verona's greatest artistic and cultural achievements came during the three centuries when the Town Council and the Scala family were in power. It was in this period that Verona's splendid townscape, which survives to this day, was mostly built. Although Verona did not lack poets and writers, the city's greatest artistic achievements were in the field of sculpture and architecture.

There are some outstanding examples of the Romanesque style in Verona such as the churches of the Holy Trinity (Santissima Trinità), St. Stephen (Santo Stefano), St. Laurenee (San Lorenzo), St. Zeno, St. John in the Valley (San Giovanni in Valle), the Lower Church of San Fermo, etc. The Gothic style is exemplified by, among the churches, Sant'Anastasia, the greater part of the Duomo, San Fermo, and among non-religious buildings by the Castelvecchio, and the Arche Scaligere, or tombs of the Scala family. There is a great deal of very impressive sculpture in Verona, by unknown or little known craftsmen and stonemasons of the 13th and 14th cents. These men were primarily inspired by the great masters Nicolo and Guglielmo, but they were also open to other influences ranging from Venetian and Byzantine to the Wiligelmic, Carolingian and Ottonian. The finest products of this group of sculptors are the magnificent doors of the Duomo and San Zeno, and the 14th cent. monument to the Scala family, towering over which stands the impressive statue of Cangrande della Scala on this horse. The earliest frescoes of note are the ones in the Chapel of St. Nazaire, (San Nazaro), painted in the 10th cent. and even these early attempts are outstanding. Later frescoes, such as the early 14th cent. ones, clearly show the influence of Giotto and examples of these are to be found in San Fermo. There was, however, no distinct "School of Verona" as such, until the middle of the 14th cent. when Turone effectively founded the Veronese "school". He was followed by Altichiero, the famous artist, who worked both in Padua and Verona. As a result of

The fifteenth-century shrine of the Virgin near the Arena "Wing".

Verona's unique position as an intermediary amongst widely diverse cultures, the city became one of the main centres of the International Gothic movement during the late 14th and 15th cents. Stefano da Verona and Pisanello were among the most outstanding painters of this period, Pisanello being a particularly brilliant medallionist.

The Renaissance movement reached Verona rather later, in the mid-15th cent., and with it came Andrea Mantegna, who had begun his painting career ten years earlier in Tuscany. From then on, all the painters working in Verona remained to a greater or lesser extent under the influence of Man-

tegna, until examples of Bellini's style and later of Giorgione and Titian started coming in from Venice. In the 14th and 15th cents., Verona produced many famous artists, such as Domenico and Francesco Morone, Liberale da Verona, Francesco Benaglio, Girolamo dai Libri, the two Caroto brothers, Francesco Bonsignori, Cavazzola, Nicolò Giolfino, Michele da Verona, to name but a few. Later artists include Francesco Torbido, Bonifacio de' Pitati, the two Brusasorcis, and Antonio Badile. During the late 16th cent., the influence of Mannerism became visible in the work of Paolo Farinati, and in the work of others of the School of Verona. This was the period in which Verona gave Venice one of her most famous sons: one of the greatest painters of the century - Paolo Caliari, called "Veronese". Fra' Giovanni, a monk belonging to the Order of the Mount of Olives, was responsible for the breathtaking wooden inlay work in the interiors of the churches of Santa Maria in Organo, and Monteoliveto Maggiore, near Siena. The sculptor Antonio Rizzo did most of his best work in Venice, but the artist whose work is most remarkable in 16th cent. Verona is the military and civilian architect Michele Sanmicheli. He worked throughout the widespread Republic of Venice, spending a good deal of time in Verona. As well as being responsible for the walls which defended the city, Sanmicheli enriched the town with graceful palaces, imposing gateways, and his masterpiece, the Cappella Pellegrini.

During the Renaissance period many of Verona's sons distinguished themselves in the arts and sciences. During the Baroque period, there was a decline in the artistic activity of both Verona and Venice. Despite this, there are many famous names which make their appearance during this period, 18th cent. Verona saw the rise of various Academies, which produced many very distinguished men.

The arrival of Napoleon and the French and the fall of the Venetian Republic at the end of the 17th cent. brought an abrupt change in the history of Verona. Many decisive battles were fought in the area around the city, including those of Arcole and Rivoli. Against the invading Jacobins, the Veronese people, true to the traditions of Venice and Catholicism, rose in a rebellion known as the "Pasque Veronesi" (Veronese Easter), so called because it took place over Easter in April 1797. Thereafter, the town was captured by the Austrians and in 1801 it was split between Austria and France. In 1805, it became a part of the Kingdom of Italy, but finally returned under Austrian domination in 1814. This marked the beginning of a long and irksome subjection to Austria. This period was, however, punctuated by bold attempts at rebellion and conspiracies, which resulted in the death of patriots such as Carlo Montanari, born in Verona and hanged at Belfiore in March 1853. This period was also punctuated by important battles which took place in the neighbourhood of the city: the battles of Santa Lucia and Custoza in 1848, San Martino and Solferino, then the Peace of Villafranca in 1859, and a second battle of Custoza in 1866. Throughout this time there was much sacrifice and boodshed, which only came to an end when the city finally became part of Italy again on the 16th October, 1866. Then began the long patient struggle to recover lost time and opportunities. Verona had to recover from the heavy military demands made upon it in the years of virtual bondage, when the city was the principal fortress of the Quadrilatero, a defensive system based on a square formation, with Verona, Peschiera, Mantua and Legnano at each corner.

The city then had to carve out a new future for itself. In 1882, it was devastated following the flooding of the River Adige. In the years 1915-1918 it was in the front line of the First World War, and was among the most badly damaged of all Italian cities. Despite the natural and man-made disasters which Verona has experienced throughout its history, it has emerged as one of the foremost cities in Italy, and looks forward to an increasingly prosperous future.

A brief glance at the culture and art of Verona during the 19th and

20th cents. shows that the town did not lag behind in modern developments and ideas. The 19th cent. saw the rise of poets such as Ippolito Pindemonte, Aleardo Aleardi and Antonio Cesari, who devoted himself to trying to improve the Italian language by attempting a revival of its Medieval purity. Other distinguished artists were architects such as Barbieri and Giullari, sculptors like Della Torre and Fraccaroli, and painters such as Canella and Cabianca. The late 19th and early 20th cents. saw an upsurge of Traditionalism in Veronese art.

The history of Verona has now reached modern times, and it is not necessary to mention a long list of important artists who are still living to prove that Verona still holds its own as an artistic and cultural centre.

The Portoni della Bra.

THE APPROACH TO THE TOWN

The most widely used and most convenient approaches to Verona are from the south, where the exits from the "Serenissima" and Brenner autostradas and the junction of two main roads, the 11 and 12, are. The approach from this direction takes the visitor past the industrial area and the exhibition grounds, and the Porta Nuova railway station. The meeting place for the traffic converging on Verona from the south is the vast Porta Nuova square just outside the circle of the walls built by the Venetians and the Austrians, which still surround the city. It is here that Verona really begins.

The massive **Porta Nuova**, through which the visitor enters this side of the city, is a monument to the genius of Michele Sanmicheli. The Porta Nuova was built between 1535 and 1540, but only part of what is now standing is original, as some of it was rebuilt by the Austrians in 1854.

Porta Nuova, by Michele Sanmicheli; below: *the "Listone della Bra".*

PIAZZA BRA

Piazza Bra is the largest square in Verona, in fact one of the most spacious and impressive in the whole of Italy. One enters the Piazza through an archway known as the **Portoni della Bra**, consisting of two huge arches surmounted by bat-

tlements which formed part of the walls built by Gian Galeazzo Visconti at the end of the 14th cent. This gateway is flanked on one side by the **Torre Pentagona**, which was also built at the end of the 14th cent. The centre of Piazza Bra is occupied by public gardens, containing a statue erected in 1883 to *Vittorio Emanuele II*, as well as a more recent one erected in honour of the *Partisans* of

Palazzo della Gran Guardia and *Palazzo Barbieri;* below: *Piazza Bra, the fountain.*

the Second World War. Many of the buildings which form three sides of the square are of great architectural importance. **The Palazzo della Gran Guardia**, the first building on the left of the "Portoni", although similar in style to the work of Sanmicheli was, in fact, built in 1610 by Domenico Curtoni. The Palace remained incomplete until 1820, and is notable for its massive bulk, as well as the forceful design of the façade, the doorway, and the windows. After the Palazzo della Gran Guardia comes the Neoclassical **Palazzo Barbieri**, otherwise known as the "Nuova Gran Guardia" which now houses the municipal offices. It was built in 1838 by G. Barbieri in the then fashionable classical style. On the left is the **Amphitheatre**. The fourth side of the square has a gracefully curving line of buildings. The line of the buildings is further emphasised by a very wide pavement, known as the **Listone**, and it is here that many of the people of Verona like to take an evening stroll. Among these build-

Entrance to the Museo Lapidario Maffeiano; below: *burial stele of husband and wife, Roman period.*

ings, the most important architecturally is the **Palazzo Guastaverza**, designed by Sanmicheli.

MUSEO LAPIDARIO MAFFEIANO

This is reached through a passage under the arcade of the Filarmonico, near the Portoni della Bra. Founded by the Veronese scholar Scipione Maffei in 1714, it is the oldest museum in Europe devoted to a collection of ancient inscriptions. In the open gallery, designed by the architect A. Pompei, there is an outstanding exhibition of stone slabs bearing inscriptions, statues, funeral urns, and bas-reliefs, most of them Etruscan, Greek or Ro-

Above: *entrance courtyard to the Museo Lapidario Maffeiano*; above, left to right: *statue of a woman* and *funerary stele*.
Facing page: *the Roman amphitheatre, better known as "Arena"*.

man, with a few Medieval fragments. The collection was catalogued and described by Maffei himself in his publication *Museum Veronense*, 1749.

TEATRO FILARMONICO

This is the chief theatre in Verona, and was one of the most important, as well as one of the most beautiful theatres in 18th cent. Italy. Built in 1716 to the design of the well known architect and stage designer Francesco Bibiena, it was destroyed by fire in 1760 and had to be completely rebuilt. The building was again destroyed in 1945, this time by bombing. Thanks to the Accademia Filarmonica Veronese, the owners of the theatre, it has now been completely restored by the architect V. Filippini, who has faithfully reproduced the beautiful 18th cent. proscenium arch.

The theatre was reopened in 1967.

THE ARENA

Fine Roman Amphitheatre, better known as the "Arena", is the most important of the monuments for which Verona is famed, and of which the city is so justly proud. Originally, the Amphitheatre stood outside the Roman walls of the city. In the 3rd cent. A.D., however, the Emperor Gallienus extended the latter to include the Arena, which is thought to have been built at the beginning of the 1st cent. In size and importance it is second only to the Colosseum in Rome. It covers an elliptical site measuring 456

Preceding pages:
bird's eye view of the Arena.
Right: *the "Wing".*
Facing page: *the interior of the Arena.*

feet by 360 feet, and the dimensions of the pit are 243 feet by 144 feet. The load-bearing structure consists of concrete and rubble with an external facing of brick and stone quarried from the hills around Verona, and this combination of materials produces an attractive colour contrast. Very nearly the whole of the perimeter wall of the building has disappeared, so that today all that remains is two tiers of arches built of rose coloured stone. Although it was never meant to be seen like this, the overall effect is extremely pleasing. In fact, most of the architecture in Verona built during the Renaissance was inspired by the Arena, the city's crowning glory. The perimeter wall fell into ruin or was deliberately destroyed over

the centuries, and all that remains today is the fragment that towers above the arena, composed of three tiers with only four arches remaining on each tier. This is known to the people of Verona as the *Ala*, or wing.

The interior of the Arena is very impressive. From the pit, one looks up at flight upon flight of giant size terraces, which sweep upwards in ever widening circles. The pride which the people of Verona take in this, the most famous of their monuments, is shown by the care lavished on the building. This pride first became evident in the late 16th cent. when a special council was set up, known as the *Conservatores Arenae*. This council was responsible for completely rebuilding the triple ring of internal arches supporting the terraces, and for the care of the 73 supports which radiate out-

wards and form the backbone of the structure.

The Amphitheatre of Verona served as a theatre for gladiatorial games, races, and other spectacular events; however, nowadays -

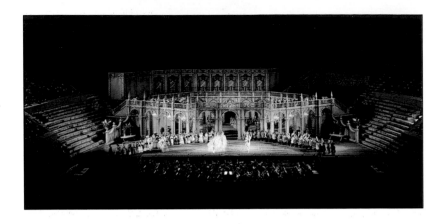

The Arena during the performance of an opera.
Facing page: *the so-called "Berlina", sixteenth-century shrine.*

from 1913 in fact - the Arena is the regular setting for splendid operatic performances.

WALLS OF GALLIENUS

From the Piazzetta (or little square) delle Mura di Gallieno, one can observe a section of the walls, which once encircled the whole town, but even this fragment is of great archaeological and historic interest, as it is all that is left of the city walls hurriedly built by the Emperor Gallienus in 265 A.D.

CHURCH OF SAN NICOLÒ
(PIAZZA SAN NICOLÒ)

This huge Baroque church was designed by Lelio Pellesina in 1627, on the site of an earlier Romanesque church; the present façade is Neoclassical in style, and originally belonged to the church of San Sebastiano which was destroyed during the war. The latter was designed by G. Barbieri in the first half of the 19th cent.

THE INTERIOR

There is a single nave, flanked by chapels, and designed in a restrained Baroque style. In the first chapel on the right there is a painting by the 17th cent. artist M. Bassetti of *St. John the Baptist*. In the second chapel on the left, *Saints Gaetano and Avellino* by the 17th cent. painter Mattia Preti.
Another painting by Bassetti, *St. Nicholas* hangs in the Sanctuary, and opposite is the *Annunciation* by Orbetto.

PALAZZETTO DEI DIAMANTI
(VIA E. NORIS)

This 16th cent. building takes its name from the diamond-shaped blocks of its stone façade. Due to extensive war damage, it had to be carefully rebuilt and restored to its original appearance.

VIA MAZZINI

Because of its central position this street is one of those most frequented both by tourists and the inhabitants of Verona.

CHURCH OF SANTA MARIA DELLA SCALA
(VIA SCALA)

Originally built by order of Cangrande I della Scala in 1325, this church has been modified over the years. The portal in the façade was made in the 16th cent. and the bell tower dates from 1362.

THE INTERIOR

It was completely rebuilt after being damaged in the war and only the outside walls are original. Cristofali designed the second chapel on the right in 1773, which contains the 14th cent. *Madonna and Saints Jerome and Zeno* fresco, which includes portraits said to be of Cangrande della Scala and his wife. A *Pentecost* by N.

Giolfino hangs above the third altar to the right. Right apse - painting of the *Crucifixion*, frescoes on the walls by Giovanni Badile, 1443, representing *Episodes from the Life of a Saint* (St. Jerome?). Left Aisle - *Tomb of Scipione Maffei*.

PIAZZA ERBE

Piazza Erbe is more or less where the *Forum* of the Roman town was. The Piazza is one of the most picturesque in Italy. It epitomises the character and atmosphere of Verona, with its lively and colourful fruit and vegetable market, covered by its world-famous giant umbrellas, the delightful variety of styles of the surrounding buildings and its historically famous and centrally placed statues. Starting from the south-western side of the square (from the corner of Via Mazzini), after the tall houses of the old Ghetto, one comes to

Piazza delle Erbe; below: **the Lion of St. Mark, on the column in the square.**
Facing page: **the Fountain of Madonna Verona.**

a low building with its battlements and porticos. It was formerly the **Domus Mercatorum,** a magnificent Romanesque building, designed in 1301 by Alberto I della Scala, and extensively altered in the 19th cent. At the far end of the square stands the impressive

Palazzo Maffei, built in 1668, a dignified structure surmounted by a balustrade supporting six statues of mythical gods and goddesses (Hercules, Jupiter, Venus, Mercury, Apollo and Minerva). Apart from its beautiful statues, there is a lovely spiral staircase in the courtyard.

To the left of Palazzo Maffei, is the square, lofty bulk of the **Torre del Gardello**. Cansignorio della Scala had it built in brick in 1370 and the bell-shaped, battlemented belfry was completed in 1626.

On the north-east side, the first building is the picturesque **Casa Mazzanti**, decorated with frescoes of mythological subjects by A. Cavalli in the 16th cent. (recently restored). Next to the Casa Mazzanti is the **Domus Nova**, whose original design has been considerably altered over the years. After the "Arco della Costa" (Arch of the Rib), so called because of the whale rib which hangs beneath it, is the **Palazzo del Comune**. The Medieval facade on this side of the Palazzo was concealed in the 19th cent. by G. Barbieri, under a Neo-classical one. The Palazzo is flanked by the **Torre dei Lamberti**, which rises 274 feet above the square, and is the tallest in Verona. It was begun in 1172 and completed in 1464 with the construction of the octagonal belfry, which still houses two ancient bells, the *Rengo* and the *Marangona*.

On the central island of the marble paved square, among the market stalls are several interesting statues. The first of them is a *Lion of St. Mark* on its 16th cent. *column*. The original statue was destroyed by the Jacobins in the 18th cent. but was replaced by a copy at the end of the 19th cent. Then we come to the *Fountain of Madonna Verona*, which Cansignorio commissioned in 1368: a column decorated with heads and symbolic figures in relief and supporting a Roman statue rises out of a circular basin from which the water overflows into a wider and lower one. Next we come to a small, square, shrine-

shaped construction once used during the ceremonies of investiture, when citizens were elected to public office. This edifice is commonly known as the "*Berlina*". Finally, at the edge of the "Toloneo", as the space occupied by the market is called, there is a pinnacled *shrine*, supported on a column (15th cent).

JULIET'S HOUSE
(VIA CAPPELLO)

Verona is world famous as the setting for Skakespeare's Romeo and Juliet. Here the love story is brought vividly to life because quite a number of buildings mentioned in the play can still be seen in Verona today. **Juliet's house,** for instance, is in Via Cappello, not far from Piazza Erbe. It is a tall building, which probably dates back to the 13th cent., with a mellow brick façade. Tradition in Verona has it that this was the house of the Capulets, the powerful Veronese family to which Juliet belonged.

From the internal courtyard, which was recently restored and around which the house is built, one can see the balcony which plays such an important part in the legend.

Top to bottom: **bronze statue of Juliet, by N. Costantini** and **the legendary balcony of Juliet's house.**

PIAZZA DEI SIGNORI

Despite its proximity to Piazza Erbe, and the fact that it almost forms part of the same complex, Piazza dei Signori is totally different in shape, style and atmosphere. This Piazza was once described, somewhat romantically, as the "drawing room" of Verona, and it is true that it is probably the most distinguished and elegant place in the whole city, perhaps because of its peace and the harmony of the surrounding buildings. Entering from Piazza Erbe, the **Palazzo del Comune** is on the right. The Romanesque façade of this tall building received considerable additions during the Renaissance period. It has the distinctive alternating bands of brick and stonework which can be considered the *leitmotiv* of the city as a whole. After a tall crenellated tower dating back to the second half of the 14th cent. is the **Palazzo del Capitano**, which has a 16th cent. façade, and a splendid entrance by Sanmicheli of the same century. In the courtyard stands the famous **Porta Bombardiera** built in 1687. The Piazza is bounded by the **Palazzo degli Scaligeri**, now the Prefecture. The original building dates from the 12th cent., but through the years it has been extensively altered. The façade

Top to bottom: *the statue of Girolamo Fracastoro* and *Piazza dei Signori*.

Porta Bombardiera.

ciations with Dante who found his "first refuge and welcome" in the home of the Scala family.

The most important monument in the Piazza dei Signori is the splendid **Loggia del Consiglio**, built between 1476 and 1493. The attribution of the building to the Veronese architect Fra' Giocondo is uncertain. This is the finest Renaissance building in Verona, where an almost Tuscan simplicity of line blends with subtle decorative work and a warmth of colour reminiscent of Venetian architecture. Statues of *Catullus, Pliny, Marcus, Vitruvius*, and *Cornelius Nepos* by Alberto da Milano crown the building.

The 18th cent. façade of the *Domus Nova*, with its grand central arch, is on the other side of the Piazza. This building houses the *Caffè Dante*, which is unique in that it still maintains the original 19th cent. interior decoration. A *statue of Dante* stands in the centre of the square, the work of Ugo Zannoni, completed in 1865.

itself, with its battlements in the style prevalent during the Ghibelline period, is the result of fairly recent restoration work. The *courtyard* is of particular interest, with its lovely Renaissance well, and with its *Gothic open gallery*, which used to be decorated with frescoes by Altichiero, painted in the 14th cent. Both this Palazzo and the nearby Church of Santa Maria Antica have close asso-

The Loggia del Consiglio, Renaissance structure, attributed to Fra' Giocondo.

THE COURTYARD OF THE MERCATO VECCHIO

This is the name given to the inner courtyard of the Palazzo del Comune, which one enters from the Piazza dei Signori, Piazza Erbe, and Via Cairoli. The square courtyard is bounded by the four inner walls of the Palazzo. the zebra striped decorative effect, obtained by using bands of brick and stone, is common to both the exterior and interior walls. The courtyard is distinguished by the bold design of its gallery, which is built in the solid Romanesque style. The elegant Gothic staircase, its two flights supported on various kinds of arches, was added in the mid-15th cent.

Tomb of Cangrande I della Scala, fourteenth-century masterpiece.

SANTA MARIA ANTICA AND THE SCALA TOMBS

The church of the Scala family was very near to their city palace, and outside it they built their family cemetery.

Their church was **Santa Maria Antica**, a very old church founded in the 7th cent. and although it is small, the interior is very beautiful. It is a splendid example of Romanesque architecture in Verona, and has the distinctive Veronese facing consisting of alternating bands of brick and stone on the outside, with cobbles included in the interior. The church tower is surmounted by a very fine square belfry, which has Gothic mullioned windows and a conical roof covered with tiles. Over the side-door there is the *tomb of Cangrande I della Scala*, who died in 1329. This also serves as a porch and is one of the best examples of 14th cent. sculpture in Verona. Under a Gothic canopy, supported by columns and topped by a pyramid shaped roof is the *tomb of Cangrande I*, decorated with sculpture in high relief. The statue of the dead prince lies on top of his tomb on a couch. The famous monument is unique, however, because of the *statue of Cangrande on horseback* which stands on top of its pyramid roof. The statue is the masterpiece of an anonymous sculptor of the 14th cent. known as the "Master of the Scala Tombs" (Maestro delle Arche Scaligere). This sculptor has portrayed the smiling horseman in vigorous and realistic style on his alert steed caparisoned for tournament. The original statue is now in the Castelvecchio Museum. The monument to Cangrande is the only one outside the marble enclosure with its splendid wrought-iron fence, which bears the emblem of the Scala family. All the other tombs are within the enclosed area, many in the shape of a sarcophagus set on the ground. One of the latter is the *tomb of Giovanni delle Scala* (who died in 1359) by Venetian stonemasons. Next to the entrance gate stands the *monument to Mastino II*, built between 1340 and 1350. It is raised on columns, and, like the earlier monument to Cangrande, the tomb lies under a Gothic canopy with decorated finials, surrounded by four small tabernacles, its pyramid crowned by the statue of the prince on horseback. The tomb itself is carved in high relief with figures of angels at each corner.

We now come to the most ornate of all the Scala family tombs - that of *Cansignorio*, who died in 1375. It is by Bonino da Campione and Gaspare Broaspini, and although it is based on the same architectural plan as the others, the workmanship is superior. The ornate decorations on the canopy were sculpted with remarkable skill and delicacy, so that the end result is like an immense and intricately elaborate ivory carving. The side tabernacles are particularly remarkable as well, of course, as the work on the tomb itself. The Scala family monuments are the supreme Gothic art achievement in Verona.

The Tomb of Cansignorio, by Bonino da Campione and Gaspare Broaspini.

Preceding page, above: *equestrian statue of Cangrande I della Scala.*
Above: *Romeo's house.*

ROMEO'S HOUSE

(VIA DELLE ARCHE SCALIGERE)

This fine Medieval building is popularly identified with the House of the Montecchi, or Montagues, Romeo's family.

The house is built of brick, and there are still traces of the original battlements, although it is now in such bad condition that no visitors are allowed into the inner courtyard.

SANT'ANASTASIA

The largest church in Verona was founded by the Dominicans in 1290 and completed in 1481. It is built on the site of an older and much smaller church likewise dedicated to St. Anastasia, of which nothing remains save the name. The facing on the lofty façade is unfinished and only covers the lower portion of the building on each side of the impressive portal. Access to the church is

Santa Anastasia.
Right above:
the apse; below:
the façade.
Facing page:
the interior.

through the mullioned twin-ogival arched doorway. The doors are framed by gracefully fluted narrow pilasters of variously coloured marble rising to form a Gothic arch above the mullioned aperture. The carving on the architrave dates from the 14th cent. and resembles the decorative work on the Scala family tombs. The fres-

coes above, however, date from the early 15th cent. and are much deteriorated. The bas-reliefs on the right pillar, representing *Episodes from the Life of St. Peter the Martyr*, are 15th cent. too.

The church possesses a high, mellow brick bell-tower built in the 15th cent.

THE INTERIOR

One of the most outstanding examples of Gothic church architecture in Verona. All the craftsmen were local. Its proportions and various elements of its design, however, are still markedly Romanesque.

The stylised paintings of plants which decorate the dome are worthy of note The floor was designed by Pietro da Porlezza in 1462. In front of the first column facing the nave are *holy water stoups* supported by human figures in a crouched sitting position, known as the "*hunchbacks*" of St. Anastasia.

THE RIGHT AISLE

The first altar, commissioned by the *Fregoso Family*, was designed by Danese Cattaneo in 1565. The second chapel dedicated to *St. Vincent Ferrer*, and attributed to Pietro da Porlezza, contains delicate marble relief work. On the upper part of the wall there is a 15th cent. fresco while the altarpiece, portraying *St. Vincent Ferrer*, is by P. Rotari (18th cent.) The third

Holy water stoup (hunchback), by Paolo Orefice (1591).

It houses five altars, including the high altar. The first chapel on the right, known as the Cavalli Chapel (*Cappella Cavalli*), contains the only non-fragmentary fresco in Verona which can be attributed with certainty to Altichiero; the mural is therefore of great interest and shows the *Cavalli Family before the Virgin*. It was painted around 1390. The frescoes on the pillar and the one in the lunette above the *Tomb of Federico Cavalli* date from the early 15th cent. and are by Martino da Verona. *St. George Saving the Princess from the Dragon*, Pisanello's most famous fresco, used to be above the arch of the second chapel in the transept, known as the *Cappella Pellegrini*. (It is now in the sacristy to the left of the transept). The walls of the chapel are completely covered with terra-

chapel is designed on the same plan as the preceding one and the lunette contains a painting of the *Descent from the Cross* by Liberale da Verona, dating from the 15th cent. The fourth chapel is reminiscent of Verona's Roman Arch of the Gavi. The altarpiece shows *St. Martin* painted by Fr. Caroto, and the painting of *Mary Magdalen* above it is by Liberale. The sixth chapel is known as the *chapel of the Crucifixion*. The bas-relief decoration is by P. da Porlezza. It contains the *Funeral monument to Gianesello da Folgaria* (about 1425) and *Pietà*, with figures in painted stone. At the end of the right *transept* is the beautiful *altar* dedicated to *St. Thomas Aquinus*. The altarpiece is by Girolamo dei Libri, and shows a *Madonna and Child with Saints*.

St. George Freeing the Princess, by Pisanello

cotta panels depicting *Scenes from the Life of Christ*, the most important work of Michele da Firenze dating from 1435.

The elegant Gothic *Main Chapel* contains the 14th cent. fresco of the *Last Judgement* on the right hand wall, and the impressive *Tomb of Cortesia Serègo* built in 1424-1429. This tomb is surrounded by an outstanding fresco depicting the *Annunciation* in the "International Gothic" style, attributed to Michele Giambono.

THE LEFT AISLE

The *Rosary Chapel* (Cappella del Rosario) is built in lavish late 16th cent. style and contains paintings by Veronese artists of the Baroque era, together with contemporary sculpture.

Over the altar, 14th cent. panel painting of the *Madonna of the Rosary*, protector of the town. Next comes the *Miniscalchi Chapel* (16th cent.); the *lunette* fresco is by Francesco Morone and the panel painting of the *Pentecost* is by N. Giolfino (16th cent.).

The third altar on the left (at the entrance) is dedicated to *St. Raymond*, and the altarpiece is a *Madonna and Saints* by D. Brusasorci (16th cent.). The second altar on the left is dedicated to *St. Erasmus*, and the altarpiece is *Christ and Saints* by Nicolò Giolfino.

The *Tomb of Guglielmo di Castelbarco* stands in the **Piazza di Sant'Anastasia** on the left of the

façade as one faces the church. It was built around 1320, and anticipates the suspended structure of the Arche Scaligere.

VIA SOTTORIVA

This street is reached by walking down beside the Church of St. Anastasia, and is one of the oldest and best preserved of all Verona's ancient streets. Most of the buildings along it date from the Middle Ages, and one side is completely composed of arcades. The 13th cent. **Casa dei Monselice** is only one of the ancient buildings which still exist in this street.

PIAZZETTA BRA MOLINARI

Situated behind the apse of St. Anastasia, this little square is laid out as a garden. From it one enjoys a lovely view over the River Adige, the Hill of St. Peter (Colle di San Pietro) and of the upper section of the Roman Theatre. In the immediate vicinity and well worth a visit, is the rambling, picturesque **Via Ponte Pietra**.

THE MODERN ART GALLERY

The beautiful **Palazzo Forti** (formerly **Palazzo Emilei**), was designed by Ignazio

Pellegrini at the end of the 18th cent. Recent restoration has brought to light important traces of the 13th cent. *Palazzo di Ezzelino*, which once stood on the site. Today, the building houses the *Modern and Contemporary Art Gallery*, where the ground floor is mainly used for special exhibitions, chiefly devoted to contemporary or modern art, whereas the beautiful rooms upstairs are generally occupied by a series of 19th and 20th cent. Veronese artists' works which have not yet been assigned a definite position and are thus exhibited in rotation in these rooms. This building used to house the Museum of the Risorgimento, now no longer in existence.

THE AREA AROUND THE DUOMO

It has been said with some justification that the real Verona, the true essence of the city, is to be found in those areas which are least likely to be visited by the tourist, who concentrates on the obvious "sights". The old quarter surrounding the Duomo, is an example of this "real" Verona which the tourist often overlooks. The streets are peaceful, sometimes patrician in character, sometimes plebeian. The buildings and palaces are of traditional design, the bricks are mellow, and the varied styles of architecture of different centuries jostle each other side

by side. There are unexpected squares and sudden, hidden alleyways, and splendid doorways - luckily one of the most outstanding of these is among the best preserved. Even the most hasty visitor cannot fail to be charmed by the atmosphere of this area which is composed of *Via Duomo, Via Ponte Pietra, Via Pigna, Stradone Arcidiacono Pacifico, Piazza Broilo and Piazza Vescovado.*

THE CATHEDRAL

Santa Maria Matricolare, the Cathedral of Verona, stands in a small square flanked by ancient buildings, which create a perfect setting for the lovely old church, that stands partly on the site of a very ancient and pre-existing basilica. It was consecrated in 1187, although building and decoration continued long after this date.

The design of the façade is unusual because of the mixture of Romanesque and Gothic elements it contains. There is a splendid *canopy* above the doorway, composed of two arches, one above the other. It is an example of the Romanesque style developed in Verona and the Po Valley, ascribed to Master Nicolò and his school, who built the entrance in 1138. The right hand side of the building, the only one completely visible, is of great interest, with its

The façade of the Cathedral with the double-arched portico.

lovely side door, as is also the **apse** with its excellent relief work executed by Veronese craftsmen. The belltower is still not complete, despite work carried out on it recently by the architect E. Fagiuoli. The 16th cent. middle section is by Sanmicheli.

THE INTERIOR

Spacious and impressive. Two lines of powerfully ribbed piers branch out to support the Gothic vaulting, dividing the nave from the aisles. The trompe-l'oeil architecture scenes painted in the first three chapels in both right and left aisles is by G. M. Falconetto and was painted in the 16th cent.

RIGHT AISLE

The second chapel contains the *Epiphany* by Liberale da Verona, and the *Descent from the Cross, with Four Saints* by N. Giolfino. The third chapel houses the 18th cent.

The portal, in the Verona Romanesque style, by Maestro Nicolò.

Transfiguration by G. B. Cignaroli and the *death mask of Pope Lucius III*, (died 1185). At the end of the right aisle, in the Cappella Mazzanti, lies the **Tomb of Saint Agatha**, a masterpiece by a follower of Bonino da Campione, dated 1353. The church's *main chapel* contains remarkable frescoes painted in the dome of the apse and on the arch. The subjects are the *Annunciation*, and the *Stories of Mary and the Prophets*, painted by Fr. Torbido in the 16th cent from sketches by Giulio Romano.

A marble choirscreen by Sanmicheli encloses the main chapel and presbytery.

The third chapel contains the *Madonna and Saints* by A. Brenzoni (1533), and the *Epitaph of Archdeacon Pacifico*, a famous Veronese personage of the 9th cent. The first (*Nichesola*) Chapel, with carved decorations by the famous Venetian architect Sansovino, contains the famous altarpiece by Titian

The interior of the Cathedral; below: *The Assumption by Titian.*

(ca. 1535), the *Assumption* (the only painting he actually worked on in Verona). Opposite to the left of the entrance, is the *Nichesola Monument,* an important work by Jacopo Sansovino.

SAN GIOVANNI IN FONTE
(NEXT TO THE DUOMO)

This little church, which was once the Baptistery of the Cathedral, was founded in the 8th and 9th cents. The existing structure which includes a nave, two aisles and three apses, dates from the early 12th cent. Only the capitals of the columns of the earlier structure are still extant.

THE INTERIOR

The church contains paintings by Veronese painters of the 16th cent. as well as the remains of 13th, 14th

Interior of San Giovanni in Fonte.

and 15th cent. frescoes. The magnificent octagonal *Baptisimal Font* (ca. 1200), one of the most outstanding examples of Medieval Veronese sculpture, stands in the centre. It is made of a single block of pink marble and around the exterior of each of the eight sides of the font are bas-reliefs with scenes from the New Testament, six of which, from the *Annunciation to the Shepherds* to the *Baptism of Christ*, bear a close resemblance to the style of Maestro Brioloto in his sculptures on the façade of San Zeno. The remaining two panels, depicting the *Annunciation and Visitation*, and the *Nativity*, are obviously by another hand, although still in Venetian Byzantine style.

CHURCH OF SANT'ELENA

In the immediate neighbour-hood of the church of San Giovanni in Fonte stands the small 12th cent. church of St. Helen. Its most important item is the 14th cent. *Crucifix*.

buildings, it is the finest Medieval cloister in Verona. It was built around 1140 in the Romanesque style and possesses two particularly beautiful tiers of arches supported on twin columns. Those on the eastern side are original, while those to the west were destroyed during the war, but have recently been faithfully restored. The traces of mosaics which can be seen on the floor of the cloister belonged to the early Christian basilica original-

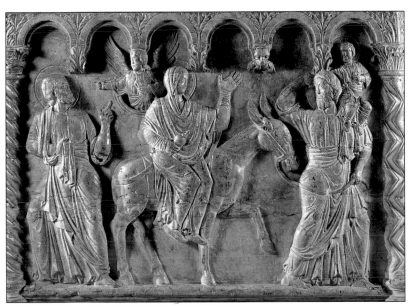

Detail of the baptismal font in San Giovanni in Fonte, example of Medieval Veronese sculpture.

CHAPTERHOUSE CLOISTERS AND CHAPTER LIBRARY

To the left, a short distance away from the Cathedral, stands the **Cloister of the Chapterhouse.** Surrounded by ancient

ly built on the site. The rest of the mosaic floor is still buried under the central lawn. From Piazza Duomo, one enters the **Chapter Library** (Biblioteca Capitolare). The Library was founded in the 5th cent. and is thus the world's oldest surviving Library and much consulted by students from every country. It contains a priceless collection, not only of printed books, but also of codices, miniatures, parchment scrolls and volumes, manuscripts, incunabula etc. (e.g.: the 5th cent. *Institutiones Gaii* and the 6th cent. *Codex Justinianeus*). The Cloister also houses the **Museo Canonicale** (Museum of the Chapterhouse), which, although small, is of great interest.

PALAZZO VESCOVILE
(PIAZZA VESCOVADO)

The Bishop's Palace has a 16th cent. façade and battlements. Over the entrance stand statues of *Sts. Michael, Peter and Paul*, and in the lunette is a painting of the *Madonna and Child* attributed to Fra Giovanni da Verona. The *courtyard* is a pastiche of styles from various centuries, and faces the apses of San Giovanni in Fonte. The crenellated tower dates from 1172. The statue of *David* is by A. Vittoria (16th cent.) The walls of the *Salone dei Vescovi* (Hall of the Bishops) are covered with 16th cent. frescoes by D. Brusasorci.

PALAZZO MINISCALCHI
(VIA GARIBALDI)

The original part of this palace is the section now facing Via San Mamaso. It is a 15th cent. construction with a frescoed façade and arched windows. In 1880, the three wings and the garden in front of them were added. It houses the *Miniscalchi Bequest*, a very valuable art collection.

PALAZZO FRANCHINI
(VIA ST.EGIDIO AND VIA EMILEI)

A fine example of late 15th cent. Gothic architecture with an attractive corner balcony, the decorated façade is of great interest. The courtyard contains a fine *well* in the Venetian style.

CHURCH OF SANT'EUFEMIA

This great church was begun in 1275, and it was eventually consecrated in 1331, but its original structure was greatly altered throughout the succeeding centuries. The fine portal is 15th cent., and there are two tall double windows. On the façade is the marble sarcophagus and the *Tomb of the Lavagnoli Family* (ca. 1550). On the left, there is the *Verita Family Tomb*. Romanesque bell-tower.

THE INTERIOR

There is a central nave with ceiling decorated with modern frescoes. Second altar on the right, Altar-

piece by F. Torbido showing *Saints Barbara, Anthony Abbot and Roch.* (16th cent.). The third altar on the right contains the *Madonna and Six Saints* by D. Brusasorci. The seventh altar on the right, *Madonna and Saint Thomas of Villanova* by Cignaroli (18th cent.). The *Chapel of the Spolverini dal Verme* contains the frescoed *Voyage of Tobias, St.*

Ursula and *Saint Lucy*, all by F. Caroto. On the left wall *Madonna and Saints* by Moretto da Brescia, and the *Crucifixion* by F. Brusasorci.

along this avenue. Unfortunately, only the left hand side of the church remains unaltered, with its bands of alternating stone, cobbles and brick.

CHURCH OF SAN GIOVANNI IN FORO
(Corso Porta Borsari)

This ancient Romanesque church stands at the top of Corso Porta Borsari as one leaves Piazza Erbe, and is only one of the many ancient buildings

PORTA BORSARI

This archway stands at the end of Corso Porta Borsari, and was the *decumano* gate of the Roman city. All one can see of the

Porta Borsari, with two passageways.

gate today is the façade, which faces towards Corso Cavour, as the building itself has now collapsed. This remnant of Roman Verona is next in importance to the Amphitheatre, and dates from the second half of the 1st cent. The gateway, which formed part of the first circle of city walls, consists of the two original arches with their lintels, tympana, and columns, surmounted by a double row of windows. The decoration on these windows inspired the architects of the Renaissance period, from Sanmicheli onwards. The gate bears an inscription dating to 245 A.D. in which Verona is given its Roman name: COLONIA VERONA AUGUSTA.

THE PALAZZI (PATRICIAN HOUSES) ON CORSO CAVOUR

In Roman times Corso Cavour was a *Via Sacra* situated outside the city walls.

LEFT SIDE

The 16th cent. **Palazzo Carnesali,** a well-proportioned building with elegant doorways and balconies. **Palazzo Scannagatti-Gobetti** is a fine example of Renaissance architecture in Verona, with fine balconies and good relief decoration in marble. **Palazzo Bevilacqua** is one of Michele Sanmicheli's masterpieces, dating from about 1530. It is thought to have formed part of

a project which was never completed by the architect. The design of the building was influenced by classical architecture, and most probably by the nearby Porta Borsari; Sanmicheli enriched the complex façade of the building with graceful sculpted decoration.

RIGHT SIDE

The impressive **Palazzo Carlotti,** dating from 1665, designed by P. Schiavi. The Neoclassical **Palazzo Portalupi** (1802), by the architect G. Pinter, now seat of the Banca d'Italia. The small **Palazzo Muselli** is an elegant example of the Baroque, distinguished by its tall chimneys in Medieval style. **Palazzo Canossa** was built to a classical design by Sanmicheli around 1530, and the loggia and statues were added in the 18th cent., together with the spacious courtyard overlooking the River Adige.

PIEVE DEI SS. APOSTOLI
(PARISH OF THE HOLY APOSTLES)
(IN PIAZZETTA SS. APOSTOLI)

The leafy, quiet piazza surrounds the monument to the Veronese poet *Aleardo Aleardi.* The ancient Pieve dei Santissimi Apostoli was consecrated in 1194. The side that flanks the square, the graceful Romanesque *bell-tower* and part of the façade still preserve their original appearance. The canopied tombs on the side were schemati-

The façade of San Lorenzo.

cally reconstructed after the war, during which they had been badly damaged. The interior still contains an important *Crucifix* and paintings by Cignani, Brusasorci and Ligozzi. Remnants of a fine 12th cent. Cloister are visible along the side of the church.

The Pieve is flanked by another ancient building: the **Church of Saints Teuteria and Tosca**, built in 751. It is partly derelict, but still of great interest because of its gracefully austere lines. See the tombs of Saints Teuteria and Tosca and two *sarcophagi* of the Bevilacqua Family.

CHURCH OF SAN LORENZO
(CORSO CAVOUR)

This is one of the most beautiful and important churches in Verona. It is built on the site of an Early Christian basilica, some fragments of which are visible from the courtyard. One enters the courtyard from Corso Cavour, passing under an archway bearing a statue of St. Laurence. It was built about 1117 and soon afterwards considerably enlarged.

This is one of the best examples of pure Romanesque style in Verona. There is a peaceful, silent atmosphere and the severity of the design is only lightened by the effect of the alternating bands of stone and brick. The graceful arches and women's gallery are supported by lofty and well-proportioned piers. Fragments of 13th cent. frescoes on the walls include huge *St. Christopher*. Over the altar is a *Madonna and Saints* by D. Brusasorci, and on the left are 16th cent. sarcophagi.

The exterior is in typical Verona Romanesque style, with alternating bands of brick and stone. The porch on the right and the belltower, which was restored quite recently, were both originally built in the second half of the 15th cent. The church has a unique feature: the two *cylindrical towers* housing the spiral staircases leading up to the women's galleries.

GAVI ARCH

This Roman arch stands in a small square overlooking the River Adige at the end of Corso Cavour, to which it was trans-

Above: *interior of the church of San Lorenzo;* left: *the Gavi Arch.*

ferred in 1930. Its original position was in the middle of the busy thoroughfare, near the clocktower of the Castelvecchio, from where it was removed and incorporated in the medieval city walls. It was broken up by the French in 1705.

CASTELVECCHIO

The massive and crenellated Castelvecchio (Old Castle), formerly known as the Castello di San Martino, was built as a stronghold by Cangrande II della Scala during the years 1354-55. Incorporated in its structure was an extensive portion of the city walls, terminating at the River Adige. The castle has had a fairly eventful history as it has survived, though not unscathed, successive dominations by various ruling families, plus the Venetians, French and Austrians. The small fort in the inner courtyard was built by Napoleon. For obvious military reasons the castle battlements and towers were cut down, not to be restored until the 1930s, when the ancient fortress was given a new role as a museum. The irregular line of the external walls is punctuated by six roofed towers, one of which, taller and more strongly fortified than the others, is known as the **Mastio** (keep). The castle walls are bounded by a deep moat through which flowed the so-called "Adigetto" (or little Adige). The interior is divided by partition walls which separate it into three court-

The exterior of the Castelvecchio.

Top to bottom: *entrance* and *interior courtyard of the Castelvecchio*.

Above: *two other views of the interior courtyard of the Castelvecchio.*
Facing page, top to bottom: *entrance* and *view of the interior of the Museum.*

yards of varying sizes. Recent excavation has unearthed some interesting remains of the castle as it originally was, such as the **Morbio Postern Gate,** part of the inner ramparts, and the remains of the tiny and ancient church of San Martino. The fort built by Napoleon underwent considerable changes between 1923 and 1926.

The Castelvecchio has been almost fully restored to its original form, thanks to restoration work begun in 1957, under the guidance of C. Scarpa and L. Magagnato.

The museum it houses is now considered one of the best laid-out museums in the whole of Europe.

The entrance to the museum is on the ground floor, with the offices and library.

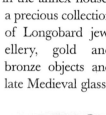

Romanesque sculpture influenced by the Veronese style. *Sarcophagus of Saints Sergius and Bacchus* (1179), 13th cent. *male figure* attributed to Brioloto and a 12th cent. ciborium in the shape of *Female figures supporting a stone slab*. The modern alcove in the annex houses a precious collection of Longobard jewellery, gold and bronze objects and late Medieval glass.

ROOM 2

14th cent. Veronese sculpture, with statues of *Saints Catherine, Cecilia, John the Baptist* and *Martha*, from the church of San Giacomo di Tomba.

The Sarcophagus of Saints Sergius and Bacchus (1173); below, left:
St Catherine of Alexandria (14th cent.) and right, **St. Cecilia (14th cent.).**
Facing page, above: ***Madonna Enthroned*** (left) and **St. Libera** (right); below:
Crucifixion and **Saint Mary, 14th-century works.**

ROOM 3

14th cent. Veronese sculpture, including *Madonna Enthroned, Crucifixion, Madonna, St. Libera.*

ROOM 4

Late 14th cent. Veronese sculpture - of note the expressive *Crucifixion* from San Giacomo di Tomba and *Mary and Martha* by the Master of Cellore.

ROOM 5

Early 15th cent. sculpture, includ-

ing panels with *Prophets,* St. *Martin* (1436) and *St. Peter enthroned.*
The **Morbio Postern Gate** leads to the Great Tower and to the other rooms.

ROOM 6

(On the other side of the wall): ancient *bells of Verona,* 14th-18th cents.

ROOM 7

(On the first floor): The Da Prato Collection of ancient firearms. This section of the Castle is known as the Royal Palace and is the best preserved.

ROOM 8

13th and 14th cent. frescoes from churches and palaces in Verona. A glass case contains 14th cent. jewellery of great beauty.

ROOM 9

Detached 14th cent. frescoes - *Madonna and Child*, the *Coronation of the Virgin*, *Crucifixion* and others.

ROOM 10

Polyptych of the Trinity and other works by Turone, an anonymous 14th cent. altar front with *The Seven Saints, Saints and a Nun*, by

Tommaso da Modena, and the *Boi Polyptych* by the school of Altichiero.

ROOM 11

Examples of the International Gothic School. This is one of the most important collections in the museum, with works by the chief exponents of the late Gothic style. The *Madonna of Humility*, *St. Jerome*, the *Resurrection*, all by Jacopo Bellini; the *Madonna of the Quail* by Pisanello, the *Madonna of the Milk* by M. Giambono, the *Madonna of the Rose Garden* and a *Madonna and Child* by Stefano da Verona. There are also works by Niccolò di Pietro Gerini, Francesco de' Franceschi and a number of *miniatures*.

ROOM 12

Dedicated to the work of foreign artists, among them Jacques Daret, Jean Patinier, Antonio Moro, Martin Van Cleef, Jean Mostaert Konrad Faber, Giacomo Jordaens, Peter Lely, Peter Paul Rubens, etc.

Crucifixion with the Virgin Mary and St. John Evangelist, from S. Giacomo di Tomba, by the Master of Cellore; below: *The Fainting Madonna (1st half 14th cent).*

ROOM 13

14th and 15th cent. paintings, including the *Death of the Virgin* by Giambono, a *Crucifixion* by Jacopo Bellini; the *Aquila Polyptych*, the *Fracanzani Ancona* (Altarpiece) *Resurrection Altarpiece* and many other paintings by Giovanni Badile.

In addition there is a great *Crucifix*, by the "Master of the Car-nation" and a fresco by followers of Altichiero.

ROOM 14

(On the top floor of the Royal Palace): Paintings by Veronese artists of the Rennaissance, including Liberale, Nicolò Giolfino, F. Verla, G. Moceto, Domenico Morone, and Giovanni Maria Falconetto.

Left: *Bell of the Gardello Tower, cast by Master Giacomo in 1370*; below: *the Arms Room.*

St. Biagio and Bishop Saint, by Bartolomeo Montagna; below: *Sambonifacio dower chest, with the Triumph of Chastity and the Triumph of Love, by Liberale da Verona.*

Facing page, above: *Madonna of the Rose Garden, by Stefano da Verona,* and, below, *Polyptych of the Trinity, by Turone.*

ROOM 15

Venetian masters of the Renaissance period: including Giovanni Bellini, with two paintings of the *Madonna and Child,* Gentile Bellini's *Crucifix of Albarelli,* Vittorio Carpaccio's *Two Saints with a Page,* and works by M. Basaiti, G. Mansueti, and B. Montagna.

ROOM 16

Important works by Veronese Renaissance painters, namely Domenico and Francesco Morone and Francesco dai Libri.

ROOM 17

Paintings by Francesco Buonsignori *Allegory of Music*, the *Dal Bovo Madonna* and *Madonna in Adoration*, as well as works by A. Vivarini and G. F. Caroto.

ROOM 18

Dedicated primarily to Liberale da Verona, this room houses his *Adoration of the Shepherds*, the *Sambonifacio Dower Chest*, the *Madonna of the Goldfinch*, and a *Nativity*.

ROOM 19

Paintings by Andrea Mantegna: *Christ Carrying the Cross, The Holy Family, Madonna and Child with St. Juliana.* Also here are a *Madonna* by C. Crivelli, a *Holy Conversation* by F. Francia and works by Girolamo dai Libri, F. Benaglio and J. da Valenza.

ROOM 20
(Next to the Mastio):

Arms and fabrics from the tomb of *Cangrande I* at Santa Maria Antica. A passageway leads back into the main museum building, past the concrete plinth with the original of the *Statue of Cangrande I on his horse,* from the cemetery of the Scala Family.

ROOM 21

Polyptych and *Four Saints* by F. Cavazzola, and other works by the same artist. The room also holds *Madon-*

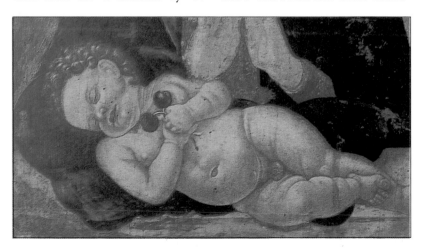

Top: ***Madonna of the Goldfinch, by Liberale da Verona;*** above: ***detail of the Madonna and Child, by Francesco Bonsignori.***

The Holy Family with a Saint, by Andrea Mantegna.

Child with a Drawing, by Francesco Caroto.

na and Saints by G. F. Caroto, *Madonna Caliari* by N. Giolfino, and finally, two panels, *A Young Monk* and *Child with a Drawing*, by Caroto.

vanni Francesco Caroto and Girolamo dai Libri, with his *Madonna Maffei.*

ROOM 22

Chiefly devoted to works by Gio-

ROOM 23

Works of the great 16th cent. Venetian artists: *Deposition*, *Bevilacqua*

Deposition, by Veronese.

Preceding page, above: ***Four Saints (late 15th cent.)*** and below, ***Madonna of the Quail, by Pisanello.***

Altarpiece, and *Portrait of Pase Guarienti,* by P. Veronese. *Nativity, Madonna of the Milk,* and *Concert of the Muses* by J. Tintoretto. *St. Dorothy* by S. del Piombo and paintings by L. Lotto and B. de' Pitati.

ROOM 24

16th and 17th cent. Veneto artists, especially Jacopo and Francesco Bassano, Paolo Farinati, Felice Brusasorci, F. Maffei, and P.Ottino. Outstanding is the splendid *Woman Taken in Adultery* by Caravaggio's Neapolitan pupil Bernardo Cavallino.

ROOM 25

Interesting paintings by Veronese and 17th cent. Venetian artists: M. Bassetti, B. Strozzi and others.

Above: ***Capriccio with Large Country House on the Bank of the Laguna, by Francesco Guardi;*** left: ***Sketch for the ceiling of the Ca' Rezzonico, by Tiepolo.***

17th and 18th cents. Venetian art. Works by B. Strozzi, A. Balestra, G. Carpioni, G. Cignaroli, and D. Feti, *Three Carmelite Monks and St. Theresa*, and *Sketch for the Ceiling of the Ca' Rezzonico*, by G.B.Tiepolo and also two *Capricci* by F. Guardi.

NOTE

The rooms of the Castelvecchio Museum are named after distinguished families or individual citizens of Verona, but these names have not been included in this guide.

PONTE SCALIGERO

This famous bridge (named after the Scala family) forms part of the complex defence system of the Castelvecchio. Although its original purpose was

Preceding page, top to bottom: *Saint Giuliana, by Andrea Mantegna; Madonna and Child, by Tintoretto* and *the interior of the Ponte Scaligero.*
Above: *view of the Ponte Scaligero.*

purely military, it is nevertheless a masterpiece of Medieval design and engineering.

Built in 1355 by Cangrande II della Scala, its architect has been identifed as Guglielmo Bevilacqua. The bridge has three great arches supported by solid turreted pylons - the widest boasting a 160 ft. span. Both the arches and the towers as well as the tall swallowtail battlements are chiefly built in brick.

The bridge presents a very imposing sight, with its glowing red brick, and the interior is no less impressive, giving fine views over the river and the city. Over the centuries, it was altered in many ways, and during the Second World War it was almost totally destroyed. However, reconstruc-tion began immediately, and the bridge is now restored to its original splendour.

CHURCH OF SAN ZENO MAGGIORE

The Basilica of San Zeno Maggiore ranks with the Amphitheatre as one of Verona's most important monuments. It is rightly considered one of the great achievements of Romanesque architecture. The present building is the third Basilica built on the same site. (The first church was built in the 4th/5th cents., the second in the 10th cent.). The present church was commenced around 1120; shortly afterwards, the builders started enlarging it and work continued until the end of the 14th cent. The roof and the apse were rebuilt in the Gothic period.

THE FAÇADE

The splendid façade is perhaps the most outstanding of this period. It dominates an enormous paved square, and is flanked by a beautiful Romanesque *belltower* from the first half of the 12th cent., of superbly masterful design. On the other side stands the red 12th cent. *tower* of the ancient monastery mentioned by Dante in Canto 18 of his "Purgatory". The weathered Veronese stone of which the church is built has a

warm golden tone, and the restrained lines of the pillars, the columns, the cornices and the gallery with its double windows give the whole façade an air of harmonious elegance. The front of the building is crowned with a tympanum decorated with marble columns, and at each side, in typical Romanesque style, the roof continues on a lower level. The lovely large circular spoked rose *window*, surrounded by allegories of "Fortune", in the centre of the façade is by Master Brioloto (reports on this artist place his activity between 1189 and 1220). The tendency nowadays is to attribute to him not only the design of the window itself, but the design of the whole complex façade. On the cornices of the sloping side roofs, a

Preceding page: *rose window on the façade of San Zeno, by Maestro Brioloto.*
Above: **Piazza S. Zeno with the basilica, the campanile and the tower.**

carved frieze by Adamino da San Giorgio (early 13th cent.).

The impressive *portal* of the church dates from about 1138, and is generally attributed to Maestro Nicolò. It was incorporated in the present façade after the demolition of the earlier façade, to which it belonged. Above the doors stands a *Porch* supported by columns on standing lions, and the lintels are decorated with carvings in relief, showing representations of the *Months of the Year*, by an unknown artist. On each side of the arch: figures of *St. John the Baptist* and *St. John the Evangelist. St. Zeno, among Infantrymen and Knights of the City Council* is sculpted in bas-relief in the lunette above the door. The

eighteen bas-relief panels on each side of the doorway also formed part of the earlier façade. They represent *scenes from the Old and the New Testament*, the *Duel between Theodoric and Odoacer*, and bottom right, *Theodoric Hunting Evil Spirits*. The latter is thought to be the work of Nicolò, while the others are attributed to his pupil Guglielmo. The doors are unique in that each one bears 24 bronze panels depicting scenes from the *Old and New Testaments and the Miracles of Saint Zeno*. These panels are enclosed in borders of varied design with heads at each corner. In addition, the border of the right-hand door has the figures of *six Saints* and a *Sculptor*, while

Top: ***bas-relief with St. Zeno among Infantrymen and Knights of the City Council, in the lunette over the entrance portal;*** above: ***detail of a caryatid in the baldachin.***

on the border of the left-hand door are 17 small panels depicting *Kings, Emperors,* and the *Virtues.* The bronze panels were transferred from the old doors when the entrance was enlarged during the early 13th cent., and as a result, a few more had to be added around this time. Most of them, however, were cast in the early 12th cent., and are attributed to a Veronese craftsman who came under the influence of Byzantine and markedly of Ottonian artists. Researchers are stil trying to identify the author of the bronze panels, but the extraordinarily vivid, "barbaric" energy of the figures, the originality and freedom of the imagery employed is a superb blend of tradition and seething renewal.

THE INTERIOR

The interior of the church is a lovely combination of Romanes-

Above and below: *details of the bas-reliefs on either side of the portal.*

que and Gothic styles. The rigorous majesty of the structural elements stresses the historical importance of this basilica. The spacious interior is divided by cruciform piers and columns supporting sweeping arches. The central arch underlines the superb, tri-sectioned keel-shaped wooden ribbed Gothic ceiling. The church is built on three different levels: the *Lower Church*, occupying about two-thirds of the building, the *Upper Church* or raised Sanctuary, and the *Crypt* beneath. The few steps leading down into the church are flanked by two *holy water stoups*. To the left: a *Baptismal Font* of monolithic design, attributed to Brioloto (12th cent.).

Descent into Hell

Christ in Glory.

Beheading of St. John

The Two Mothers.

Expulsion from Eden.

First Labors and Fratricide.

Head on the right-hand door.

St. Zeno and the Messengers of Gallienus.

RIGHT AISLE

The walls and are covered with 13th and 14th cent. frescoes, of great importance in the history of Veronese art of this period. They represent, among others, the following - *St. Christopher* (about 1300) and the *Madonna Enthroned*, by the "Second Master of San Zeno", *Crucifixion* and *St. Stephen*, by the "First Master of San Zeno". Along the staircase and the wall of the raised Sanctuary are the *Madonna* by Martino da Verona, *St. George* by the "Second Master of San Zeno", and the *Baptism* and *Resurrection of Lazarus*, (13th cent.) and others. First altar on the right: *Madonna and Saints* by Fr. Torbido (16th cent.). Second altar on the right: built of marble taken from a 13th cent. porch.

THE SANCTUARY

Statues of *Christ* and the *Apostles* by a local sculptor who was influ-

enced by the Saxon school, stand along the top of the iconostasis or balustrade. At the top of the right wall is a votive fresco dating from 1397 (School of Altichiero). The *Main Chapel*, constructed by Giovanni and Nicolò da Ferrara in 1386-1398, is decorated with frescoes by Martino da Verona. On the high altar stands the *Triptych*, with *Madonna and Saints*, by Andrea Mantegna, painted between 1457 and 1459.

In the left apse stands an impressive statue of *Saint Zeno*. It is made of polychrome marble by an unknown sculptor of the early 14th cent., and is much loved by the people of Verona. Next to the Sacristy door stands the *Statue of St. Proculus* by Giovanni da Verona (1392). On the wall is a *Crucifixion* which shows the influence of Altichiero, and two other versions of the *Crucifixion* by Turone and by the "Second Master of San Zeno". This wall also bears traces of many other frescoes.

The interior of San Zeno.

THE CRYPT

A broad staircase leads down to the crypt. The arches are decorated with friezes in relief, by Adamino da San Giorgio dating to 1225 (probably the year when the crypt was completed). The arches and vaults of the crypt are supported by 49 columns, whose capitals are of great interest as each one is different. The central apse contains the urn holding the holy *body of Saint Zeno*. The crypt also contains several other sarcophagi, in particular those of *St. Lupicillius, St. Lucillius* and *St. Crescentian* (12th and 13th cents.).

LEFT AISLE

Baroque altar dedicated to *Our Lady of Sorrows*. At the end of the aisle, next to the entrance, stands the great

Two details of the Triptych with the Madonna and Saints by Andrea Mantegna.

monolithic *porphyry bowl,* probably of Roman origin. Legend, however, has it that the bowl was brought here by the devil. On the wall is the great *Crucifix* attributed to the Paduan artist, Guariento, and it is here that the "*Carroccio*" of the Veronese Commune was kept - when not in use - in the Middle Ages. The "*Carroccio*" was the war chariot on which the standard of the Free Commune of Verona was born to the battle-field.

Top: *Madonna Enthroned, by the Second Master of St. Zeno*; above, left: *statue of St. Zeno by unknown sculptor (14th cent.)* and, right, *Madonna and Saints, by F. Torbido*; right: *shrine in the cloister.*

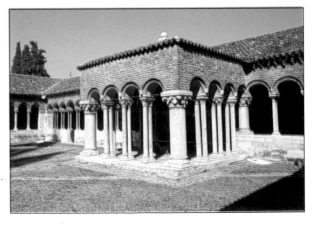

The apse and bell tower of San Zeno.

CLOISTERS

One enters the cloisters from the left aisle of the basilica. The effect is one of spaciousness, as the covered walks surround a large open grassy square. The arches on two of the opposing sides of the cloisters are ogival, while those on the other two sides are rounded. Slim double columns support the arches. A charming, open shrine with piers and columns projects from one of the sides of the cloister, which also houses stone fragments and tombs. On the eastern side is the **Chapel of St. Benedict**, once probably a Roman hypogeum, or underground burial chamber, decorated with frescoes by the School of Giotto.

Right: *entrance to San Bernardino*. Facing page: *the cloister.*

SAN BERNARDINO

It used to belong to the Franciscan Order and was founded in 1451 and completed in 1466. It is preceded by a cloister. The façade is brick and has pointed Gothic windows. *Statues of Franciscan Saints* stand above the lunette that crowns the main entrance (1474), whereas the lunette itself contains a mural of *St. Francis Receiving the Stigmata.*

THE INTERIOR

There is a single nave, a feature which is often found in Franciscan churches, as well as a side aisle and chapel on the right of the church First chapel on the right: frescoes on the walls of *Episodes from the Life of St. John the Evangelist* by N. Giolfino, who also painted the *Episodes from the Life of St. Francis* on the ceiling vault. Over the altar hangs a copy of the original painting by Cavazzola now in Castelvecchio. Second chapel on the right: *Madonna and Child with Saints*, by F. Bonsignori. Fourth chapel on the right: Frescoes by Dom. and Fr. Morone: The marble altarpiece depicts *Franciscan Saints*. Fifth chapel on the right: *The Crucifixion*, a masterpiece by Fr. Morone dating from 1498. Also, *Mary and Jesus* by Fr. Caroto, the *Resurrection of Lazarus* by A. Badile, and the *Story of the Passion*, by N. Giolfino. The *Deposition from the Cross* is a copy of the Cavazzola original now in Castelvecchio. Behind an iron railing stands a

group in polychrome stone, representing the *Lamentation over the Body of Christ*. **Cappella Pellegrini** (entrance to the right of the nave) built by Michele Sanmicheli around 1527 for Margherita Pellegrini. Sanmicheli used a centralized plan for his masterpiece. Lovely spatial proportions flow in classical stately harmony. There are two orders, with a coffered dome supported by a drum (tiburium). The door and three altars open off the lower order. Niches and three-mullioned windows with columns succeed each other in the upper order. A *Madonna and Child with St Anne* by B. India (1579) above the altar with *The Eternal Father with Sts. Joseph and Joachim* by Ottino (17th cent.) The *Main Chapel* frescoes by Michele da Verona were lost forever due to bombing.

The 1481 organ is beautifully decorated by Domenico Morone. The first altar is dedicated to the *Brasavola Family* and was designed by Fr. Bibiena in the 18th cent.. The altarpiece depicting *St. Peter of Alcantara* is by A. Balestra.

A door in the left-hand wall of the church leads to a graceful 15th cent. cloister. The lunettes in the cloisters are decorated with 15th and 16th cent. frescoes. The main cloisters give access to the ancient **Library** of the Monastery, completely covered with frescoes in 1503 by Domenico and Francesco Morone. The painting on the end wall depicts the *Madonna Enthroned* surrounded by members of the Sagramoso Family; on the side walls: *Saints and Famous Members of the Franciscan Order*.

Porta Palio; below: **the church of the Santissima Trinità.**

PORTA PALIO

This gateway takes its name from a "*Palio*" or horse-race which used to be run in the vicinity, mentioned by Dante in Canto 15 of the "Inferno". It was once known as the Porta di San Sisto and is Sanmicheli's master-piece in his capacity as a military architect. The outer façade is built of smooth square-hewn stones rigorously partitioned by paired columns, while the inner consists of five openings, in which classical simplicity merges with delightful Mannerist decoration. Behind the arches is a gallery. The gateway was built between 1542 and 1557.

CHURCH OF THE SANTISSIMA TRINITÀ

An example of the Veronese Romanesque style. The church was founded in 1073 c., and consecrated in 1117. Only the northern apse remains of the earlier building: the porch, the other apses, and the belltower were built around 1130.

The square bell-tower, with its brick and thinly banded stone facing and the elegant, three-mullioned windows of the bell-chamber is supposed to have inspired the builders of St. Zeno.

Above, left: *sarcophagus of Antonia da Sesso (1421)*, and right, *interior of the church of Ss. Trinità.* Left: *cloister of San Francesco al Corso.*

Juliet's Tomb.

Annunciation by Louis-Dorigny;
right: **detail of St. Catherine of
Alexandria, by F. Caroto**

JULIET'S
TOMB
(VIA DEL PONTIERE)

The final goal of the pilgrim in search of Shakespeare's Romeo and Juliet is Juliet's tomb

Above: *Adoration of the Magi, by Antonio Palma*; center, left: *San Celso, fresco by a 12th cent. Veronese painter*; below left: *The Orgy, by Torquato della Torre* and, right, *Washing of the Feet, by F. Caroto. (Museo degli Affreschi dedicated to G. B. Cavalcaselle).*

The apse of San Fermo Maggiore.

in the picturesque former monastery of the Capuchins. Only the *cloisters* and the Baroque *Chapel of St. Francis* remain. The empty sarcophagus lies in a dimly lit crypt, and only reached this resting place after many vicissitudes. A long, but disputed tradition has it that this is the tomb of Shakespeare's heroine.

CHURCH OF SAN FERMO MAGGIORE

In ancient times a small chapel stood on the banks of the river Adige, near the spot where St. Fermo and St. Rustico were martyred. It was rebuilt in the 8th cent. and in the 9th cent., the Benedictine

The façade of San Fermo Maggiore.

Friars began work on a much larger structure in which, from the start, one of the two churches erected on the site, was intended to be built above the other. The lower church, the two lesser apses and the bell-tower which was not completed until the 13h cent. all belong to the Benedictine project. The date 1065 which appears in the lower church, probably refers to the year in which the Benedictine part was started, whereas the building was restructured and given its present appearance by the Franciscans, who took over the complex after 1313. The great Gothic upper nave and the splendid apsidal complex were built above the pre-existing Romanesque

lower church. The two styles merge into each other harmoniously, thanks to the unity of the colour-scheme maintained throughout the complex. The absidal sector of the upper church has delightful inter-woven decorations and richly ornamented arches.

THE FAÇADE

The varied openings in the façade progress, diminishing in scale, up to the point of the roof, from the great recessed Main Door, flanked by two *Porched Tombs* (left: *Monument to Aventino Fracastoro* - doctor to the Scala family - who died in 1368; the frescoes which used to decorated the tomb are now in the

Top to bottom: *San Fermo Maggiore from the Ponte delle Navi* and *funeral monument of Aventino Fracastoro, on the façade of the church.*

museum of Castelvecchio). Right: the porched *Tomb of Giovanni da Tolentino)* and by mullioned ogival windows, to a great four-mullioned ogival window topped by a smaller three-mullioned window and two round port windows, above which a series of pensile arches define the simple gable-shaped top of the façade.

The usual entrance to the church is on the left side where a staircase, covered by a massive porch, leads up to the door. 13th cent. frescoes in the lunette (the one on the left by Fr. Morone, 1523).

Of typical Franciscan design, with a single nave, it has a 14th cent. multi-keel-shaped wooden ribbed ceiling, decorated with images of *Saints*. The church is primarily famous for the quality and number of its 14th and 15th cent. frescoes. In the lunette above the main door is the *Crucifixion*, attributed to Turone. On the opposite wall are fragmentary 14th and 15th cent. frescoes, including a *Last Judgement* by Martino da Verona.

Interior of San Fermo Maggiore.

14th cent. fresco representing the *Martyrdom of Franciscan Friars*. Above the 16th cent. *Nichesola Altar* is a *Madonna and Saints* by S. Creara, while the lunette is by D. Brusasorci. The detached fresco, *Angels with a Scroll*, is by Stefano da Verona. The **Pulpit** (1360) was commissioned by a lawyer, Barnaba da Morano, and is surmounted by a Gothic canopy. The frescoes surrounding it are by Martino da Verona. The *Annunciation* - a fresco - on the upper section of the wall, clearly reveals Giotto's influence. On the walls of the Brenzoni Chapel (15th cent.) are the *Tomb of Bernardo Brenzoni* (died 1494), and the *Funeral Monument of Barnaba da Morano*, decorated with statues and fine reliefs, probably by Venetian artists. The third altar, known as the *Saraina* (16th cent.), used to be in the Church of the Holy Trinity (Santissima Trinita). On the altar front is a 15th cent. *Deposition*. The fine altarpiece shows *The Holy Trinity, Madonna and Saints* and is by Fr. Torbido. The fifth altar was architecturally inspired by the Roman Gavi Arch.

RIGHT APSE

Crucifixion, by D. Brusasorci. Then comes the *Main Chapel*, highlight of the Basilica, in front of which there is a semi-circular screen (1523). Above the triumphal arch, frescoes (about 1314), which depict the kneeling figures of *Prior Daniele Gusmerio* and *Guglielmo di Castelbarco*, and which clearly reveal the influence of Giotto. There are other important 14th cent. frescoes on the wall: the *Coronation of the Virgin*, *Adoration of the Magi* and the *Stories of the Franciscan Friars*. Behind the 18th cent. main chapel altar there are rare wooden choirstalls (15th cent.). The vault of the ceiling above the apse is decorated with 14th cent. frescoes, depicting the *Symbols of the Four Evangelists*. Above the altar in the nearby *Chapel of St. Anthony* hangs Liberale da Verona's outstanding *Saints Anthony, Nicholas and Augus-*

Fourteenth-century pulpit with frescoes by Martino da Verona.

tine. Monument to the Della Torre Family, in the rectangular chapel beside the left wall, a splendid example of the sculpture of A. Briosco, called "II Riccio", with richly carved marble sections and superb bas-reliefs in bronze. The originals of the bronze reliefs - now in the Louvre, in Paris - are replaced by copies.

THE LEFT WALL

The Baroque *Lady Chapel,* with a *Madonna with Saints,* a masterpiece

by Fr. Caroto above the altar. A 1363 fresco of the *Crucifixion* above the side door. The 1535 *Chapel of the Helmsmen* (Cappella dei Nocchieri) contains *Saints Nicholas, Augustine and Anthony Abbot,* by Battista Dal Moro, the famous *Monument to Nicolò Brenzoni* by the Florentine artist Nanni di Bartolo, who sculpted a *Resurrection* all around the urn between 1424 and 1426. In these years the great Pisanello painted one of his most famous frescoes on the surrounding wall - the outstanding *Annunciation.* Above it, subtly harmonising with the architectural lines, are the figures of the *Almighty* and the *Archangels Raphael* and *Michael.* This fresco is a masterpiece of the artist's early period and is a work of great importance in the study of northern Italian Gothic art.

Left to right: ***Funeral monument to Nicolò Brenzoni, by Nanni di Bartolo*** and *the lower church of San Fermo Maggiore.*

Built around 1065 this church is an outstanding and rare example of early Veronese Romanesque architecture. The great nave, separated from the aisles by piers, has double arches supported by a row of smaller piers. The varied shapes of the ancient capitals are of note, together with the 13th and 14th cent. frescoes on the walls and piers.

PORTA DEI LEONI
(THE LION GATE) IN VIA LEONI

Yet another monument bequeathed by the Romans, dating from the middle of the 1st century B.C. It was once part of the ancient city walls, and was drastically altered about a hundred years after its construction. It consisted of

The Lion Gate (Porta dei Leoni).

The most recent excavations near the Porta dei Leoni.

two arches topped by a tympanum and flanked by columns, above which rose a series of arched windows, and finally a large exedra. The rear of the existing section is concealed by a building immediately behind it, but the visible part corresponds more or less to the centre of the original gate. This gate, which is one of the most precious mementos of Roman Verona, was much admired by the artists of the Renaissance period for its perfect proportions and the beauty of its ornamentation. Recent thorough archaeological digs, the results of which are clearly visible from the street, have revealed the base of the ancient Roman gateway, extensive sections of the original road surface and the polygonal base of one of the great corner towers, defending the gateway.

THE CITY LIBRARY
(BIBLIOTECA CIVICA IN VIA CAPPELLO)

This library, founded in 1792, is one of the most important in Italy.

It contains about half a million books, 1,209 incunabula, and over 3,700 manuscripts. Many of the incunabula are very rare and of great value. In addition, there are a number of ancient documents, illuminated manuscripts, over 2,000 prints and drawings, and a fine collection of over 30,000 autographs. The *Ancient City Archives* are also stored here. In the foyer is a comprehensive array of portraits (busts and medals) of famous Veronese men through the ages, known as the *Protomoteca*.

PALAZZO POMPEI MUSEUM OF NATURAL HISTORY
(LUNGADIGE PORTA VITTORIA)

Formerly known as Palazzo Lavezola, it was built by the architect Sanmicheli, between about 1530 and 1550, when his reputation was already firmly established. It is one of his great works, and shows a very strong classical influence, despite concessions to

Top to bottom: *fossil trunk; façade of the Palazzo Pompei, by Sanmicheli, seat of the Museum of Natural History* and *the interior courtyard of the building.*

the style of the time and the purpose of the building. The impressive facade, divided into two storeys, and the well-proportioned internal courtyard are of particular interest.

This Palazzo has long housed the **Museum of Natural History**, which

Top to bottom: room of the *Eocene fossils; showcase in the Room of Mushrooms* and *exposition of stratigraphic geology.*

Showcase in the Room of Rocks; below: ***Dombeyopsis;*** bottom, left to right: ***Mammoth, in the Quaternary Hall*** and ***Papagoite.*** Facing page: ***Scatophagus Frontalis.***

is famous throughout Italy and Europe.

There are over 20 rooms, containing rare collections, and the following fields are represented - mineralogy, palaeontology, biology, ornithology, icthyology, entomology, etc.

These are some of the more important rooms: **Room I** contains a very fine collection of *Eocene fossils* from the Bolca region. This includes a large number of animal and plant species which existed more than 30 million years ago. **Rooms II** and **III** are dedicated to collections of *minerals* and *stones*. **Rooms V, VI, VII,** and **VIII** are devoted to *mammals*. **Rooms IX, X, XI** and **XII** are devoted to all aspects of *ornithology*. **Rooms XIII** and **XIV** contain exhibitions of

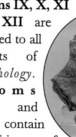

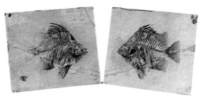

fish, *reptiles* and *amphibians*. The collection of *insects* in **Room XV** is of great interest. The remaining rooms deal with *invertebrates*, *palaeontology*, and *prehistory*, among other subjects.

CIMITERO MONUMENTALE

The city's cemetery was designed by G. Barbieri in 1828 in Neoclassical style, and is one of the most remarkable Italian cemeteries. The old part is a square flanked by buildings and Doric colonnades, and contains plentiful examples of 19th and early 20th cent. commemorative sculpture.

CHURCH OF SAN PAOLO DI CAMPO MARZO
(VIA DELL'ARTIGLIERE)

A church of 18th cent. design, it was largely rebuilt after damage. It houses several important works by Veronese Renaissance artists, such as the *Giuliari Altarpiece* by Girolamo dai Libri (fourth altar on the right), *Madonna and Child with Saints*, by Paolo Veronese, and the *Madonna Enthroned among Saints*, by G.F. Caroto, which hangs in the apse.

PALAZZO GIULIARI THE UNIVERSITY
(VIA DELL'ARTIGLIERE)

This is one of the finest 18th cent. buildings in Verona designed by the architect Ignazio Pellegrini who worked at the end of the 18th cent. The staircase in the foyer and the graceful central courtyard are very striking. In the courtyard there are traces of an earlier 16th cent. construction. The building has been recently restored and now it houses the central core of the University of Verona, namely the **Faculties** of *Economics, and Business Studies, Languages, Teacher training*, which also occupy an efficient modern building in the same street. The *Medical Faculty*, however, is housed in a large building which has recently been built in the southeastern part of the city.

CHURCH OF SANTI NAZARO E CELSO
(LARGO SAN NAZARO)

This church, built between 1464 and 1483, was once part of a Benedictine monastery. A large cloistered courtyard in front has an imposing entrance built in 1688.

THE INTERIOR

A main nave flanked by two aisles with three apses.

Entrance portal to the courtyard in front of the church of Santi Nazaro e Celso

RIGHT AISLE

The *Annunciation*, by P. Farinati (1557) hangs above the second altar. *Adam and Eve* in the lunette are by the same painter. *Ecce Homo*, by O. Flacco, above the fourth altar.

SACRISTY

The 15th cent. wall *cupboards* are decorated with marquetry. There is a 15th cent. triptych depicting the *Pietà* and *Saints Benedict and Francis*. The *Madonna and Saints* is by F. Brusasorci. The sections of a polyptych by Bartolomeo Montagna show *Saints Blaise and Juliana* and *Christ on the Sepulchre*.

The **Main Chapel** contains impressive *frescoes* and four paintings depicting *Episodes from the Life of St. Celsus* by P. Farinati. There are another two pieces by Montagna, representing *Saints Benedict* and *John the Baptist*, and *Saints Nazarus and Celsus*.

The **Chapel of San Biagio**, in the left transept, was built by the architect Beltramo di Valsolda in 1488, and consecrated in 1529. Above the main arch is a painting of the *Annunciation* by P. Cavazzola (1510). There is a splendid marble altar with the *Sarcophagus of Saints Blaise and Juliana* by Bernardino Panteo (1508), altarpiece by Fr. Bonsigno-rio (the *Martyrdom of Two Saints*, and a *predella* by Girolamo dai Libri).

LEFT AISLE

The fifth chapel contains the *Madonna and Saints* by Dom. Brusasorci In the third chapel there is the *Miracle of Saint Maurus* by G. Carpioni, and the *Madonna in Glory with Saints* by Antonio Badile is in the second chapel.

Façade of the church of Santi Nazaro e Celso.

A few pictures of the Giusti Gardens, a splendid example of a late Renaissance Italian garden.

GIUSTI GARDENS

This garden belongs to the 16th cent. **Palazzo Giusti**. It is one of the finest late Renaissance gardens in the whole of Italy, and dates from 1580. It is divided into two sections - the lower part being in the Italian style. The layout is spacious, with flower beds, a maze, statues, fountains ecc., and a cypress avenue winding up the small hill topped by the Church of San Zeno in Monte, which was much admired by Goethe. There is a tower-shaped building with a winding

CHURCH OF SANTA MARIA IN ORGANO

(PIAZZA SANTA MARIA IN ORGANO)

This church belonged to the monks of the Order of the Mount of Olives, and was redesigned in its present form in 1481. The lower part of the façade was built over an older original, and is attributed to Sanmicheli. The belltower, however, with its domed top, was designed by Fra Giovanni da Verona.

Another view of the Giusti Gardens; below: *the façade of Santa Maria in Organo*

THE INTERIOR

It is in Renaissance style, and has a nave, two aisles and a raised presbytery. The walls of the central nave are decorated with frescoes depicting *Stories from the Old Testament*, those

staircase and a platform on top, from which one enjoys a magnificent view over the city.

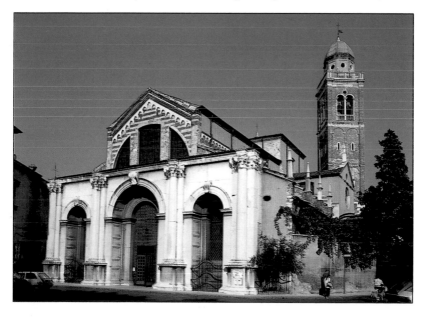

Above: *the choir of Santa Maria in Organo;* above: *example of wooden marquetry on the choir stalls.*

on the right by Francesco Caroto, and those on the left by N. Giolfino.

Madonna and Saints by Antonio Balestra in the first chapel and the *Journey of St. Joseph* by G.B. Pittoni (18 cent.). *St. Michael* by P. Farinati in the second chapel.

In the chapel opening off the end wall, on the right, flanked by frescoes by Cavazzola, *Santa Francesca Romana,* an altarpiece by Guercino (1639). The chapel to the right of the main chapel contains frescoes by N. Giolfino, and Cavazzola's *Annunciation.* In the left chapel are *frescoes* by D. Brusasorci and *St. Benedict* by S. Brentana.

The Main Chapel: paintings of the *Massacre of the Innocents* and *Episodes from the Lives of Saints Gregory and Peter* by P. Farinati. Lower down, on one side, is a series of little *Landscapes* by Domenico Brusasorci.

In this part of the church are the greatest works of Fra Giovanni da Verona - the superb multi-coloured *wooden marquetry choir stalls,* some of the finest of their kind in Italy. They were done in the late years of the 15th cent. and in the early 16th cent. and consist of two rows of choir stalls in the lovely *Choir*. Fra Giovanni was the architect of the **Sacristy** (1504) where he also decorated the cupboards. The beautiful *candelabrum* of carved wood and the *lectern* which stand in the Choir are also by Fra Giovanni.

The frescoes in the sacristy depicting *Popes and Benedictine Monks* are by Domenico and Francesco Morone. The *Landscapes* and the lower portions of the wall cupboards are by D. Brusasorci. The altarpiece depicting *Saints Anthony and Francis* is by Orbetto. In a room near the Sacristy is a 13th cent. wooden sculpture of *Christ Riding on an Ass*.

LEFT AISLE

Fourth chapel, *Madonna and Saints* by Savoldo. Third chapel, *Madonna with Saints Augustine and Zeno*, F. Morone, 1503.

THE LOWER CHURCH

This is a particularly interesting example of early Romanesque Veronese architecture. It has a nave and two aisles. An important 14th cent. marble polyptych depicting *Madonna and Saints* is on the altar in the apse.

CHURCH OF SAN GIOVANNI IN VALLE
(IN VIA SAN GIOVANNI IN VALLE)

This very ancient church was rebuilt after the earthquake of 1117, and was again

The church of San Giovanni in Valle.

badly damaged during the last war. It has a nave, two aisles and three apses, and is built entirely of stone. It was of fundamental importance in the development of the Veronese Romanesque style, and many similar churches were modelled on it.

THE FAÇADE

Severe and simple, it has side windows and a central mullioned window. The 15th cent. portal is of marble, covered by a porch. In the lunette is an important fresco by Stefano da Verona, depicting the *Madonna and Saints*. The belltower is Romanesque, with an upper section added in the 18th cent. The remains of the cloister, along the right hand side of the church, are Romanesque like the tombstones.

THE INTERIOR

The atmosphere is particularly fascinating, with a narrow central nave in striking contrast with the wider side-aisles from which it is divided by a series of piers and columns with Corinthian capitals. The ceiling is supported by wooden cross-beams. A 17th cent. staircase leads up to the raised **presbytery**.

The **Crypt** is reached from the presbytery, and has three aisles as well and contains many traces of the original church. There are two rare examples of Early Christian sculpture - both *Sarcophagi*. The first, of *Saints Jude and Taddeus*,

bears fine reliefs on the sides, and a lid added in 1395. The second, probably of Roman origin, has fluted sides, and niches containing the figures of a husband and wife, with *Saints Peter and Paul* on the sides.

CHURCH OF SAN TOMASO CANTUARIENSE
(PIAZZA SAN TOMASO)

It was built in the 15th cent. on the site of two earlier churches, and in 1504, although still incomplete, it was dedicated to Saint Thomas à Becket, archbishop of Canterbury.

THE FAÇADE

Has a fine entrance and lofty Gothic windows. The 15th cent. belltower has a tall conical spire.

THE INTERIOR

This is designed around a single nave, with a roof of wooden beams. The presbytery section, built in the 16th cent., was designed by Sanmicheli who is buried in this church.

THE RIGHT WALL

The second altar houses *The Glory of St Mary Magdalen* by Orbetto. 17th cent. *Annunciation* by Sante Creàra above the third altar. *Saints Rocco, Sebastian and Onofrio* by Girolamo dai Libri above the fourth altar.

THE PRESBITERY

In the right hand chapel a 15th cent. wooden *Crucifix*. In the apse containing the high altar: the *Madonna and Saints* by D. Brusasorci. Left: the great *Baroque Organ*, played on by Mozart in 1769.

THE LEFT WALL

Madonna and Saints by P. Farinati, above the third altar. *Saints John the Baptist, Peter and Paul*, attributed to Torbido, above the second altar. *Madonna and Saints*, above the first altar.

Entrance to the Roman Theatre.

THE ROMAN THEATRE

This Roman Theatre, which is superbly positioned on the banks of the river Adige, was built in the second half of the 1st cent. B.C. Successive constructions caused the theatre to disappear. The excavations which brought it to light were commenced by the archaeologist Andrea Monga in the middle of the 19th cent. and were only finished comparatively recently. The theatre contains semicircular tiers of seats, partly rebuilt. The *stage*, which has only been partly recovered, is flanked by the impressive ruins of the wings Unfortunately, very little remains of the imposmg façade which once faced the river Adige. Set against the green tufa hills, crowned by the ancient Monastery of St. Jerome, the theatre is very impressive. Above the last tier of seats to the left is a *loggia* with marble columns which once formed part of the theatre, though it seems unlikely that this was its original position.

An unusual feature is the wide, deep trench dug into the tufa behind the theatre to separate it from the mountain side.

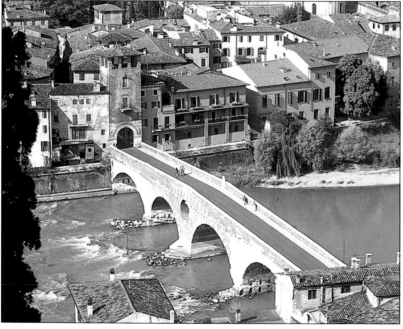

Top to bottom: *entrance to the Theatre* and *the Ponte Pietra, seen from the Theatre.*

The tiers of the Roman Theatre and *the church of Santi Siro e Libera.*

Overall view of the Roman Theatre; below, right: **bronze portrait of Augustan period.**

SAINTS SIRUS AND LIBERA

Standing on the eastern side of the theatre, it is the only remaining building of the many which were built here over the years. It was founded in the 10th cent. and was remodeled over the centuries, especially in the 17th cent. A double Baroque staircase leads up to the church, but the door and porch, and the *statue of Saint Libera* in the lunette all date to the 14th cent. Items of interest in the church include the following: an 18th cent. *Madonna and St. Gaetano* by Giambettino Cignaroli, in the first chapel on the left, the very fine *High Altar* decorated with inlaid marble panels and statues, the splendid *choir stalls* by three Germans: Kraft, Petendorf and Siut (1717-1720). There is also a painting of the *Annunciation* by Ridolfi, and a *Bust of Pope Clement XIII* above the door.

ARCHAEOLOGICAL MUSEUM

Access to this museum is by lift from the Roman Theatre (ask the Custodian)
The museum occupies part of what was once the Monastery of St. Jerome. It offers the visitor a fund of information essential to an understanding of Verona in Roman times.

Top to bottom: *Room of the Inscriptions* and *a room in the Museum*.

Top to bottom: *mosaics with scenes of gladiatorial combat (1st cent. A.D.)* and *a room in the Archaeological Museum*; below: *Two-faced Herm.*

ROOM I (THE NEW ROOM)

Important mosaics among which *scenes of gladiatorial combat* dating from the 1st cent. A.D. The sculpture includes the *Head of a Prince of the Julio-Claudian Family.* and a *Bust of a Man in Armour,* both dating from the 1st cent. The glass showcases contain a fine collection of pottery.

ROOM II, III AND IV (MONKS' CELLS)

Sculpture, bronzes, glass etc. The bronzes include a *statuette of Tiberius,* a *portrait of the Augustan era,* and a *two-faced herm.*

Cloister of San Girolamo; below: **bust of a man in armour, of Roman period.**

CORRIDOR

Roman sculpture, the most important of which is a statue of *Menander*. This is a Roman copy of the Julio-Claudian period, of a Greek original dating from the 3rd cent. B.C.

REFECTORY

Contains sculpture, urns from Volterra, inscribed gravestones, and mosaics. Among the sculptures is a *Seated*

Female Figure. This is a Roman 2nd cent. copy of the Venus of the Garden, a Greek statue of the period of Phidias. Also of note are a *Statue of a Man*, which is a Roman copy of a 4th cent. Greek statue, and a *Zeus*, also copied from a Greek original.

COURTYARD AND CLOISTER OF ST. JEROME

Roman sarcophagi and Veronese tombs.

Interior of the church of San Girolamo; below, left to right: ***Head of a Satyr*** and ***the Venus of the Gardens.***

CHURCH OF ST. JEROME

An early Christian pavement from St. Stephen is preserved here. The triumphal arch is decorated with a fresco by Caroto. *The Annunciation* (1508), and a 15th cent. *triptych* above the altar. To the right of the altar is a 4th cent. statue of the *Good Shepherd.*

THE SECOND CLOISTER

This was damaged in the 18th cent. Fragments of sarcophagi are preserved here, together with a 2nd cent. *two-faced herm,* a *Head of Heracles* and others. Finally there is the **Nymphaion**, a part of the Roman building which probably once had some connection with the Theatre below.

PONTE PIETRA

Verona had two bridges in Roman times, and this one, which was formerly known as the *Pons Marmoreus*, is the only one that remains. Fragments of the other one, known as the *Postumio*, are visible on the banks of the river near the Church of St. Anastasia. Ponte Pietra dates from the Pre-Augustan period, and has five arches. The arch next to the right hand bank was rebuilt in 1298, together with

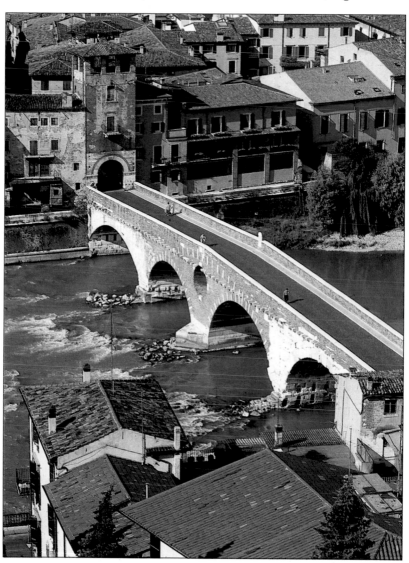

View of the Ponte Pietra.

Top to bottom: *the Ponte Pietra* and *the watch tower.*

the tall watch tower, by Alberto della Scala. The contrast between the material used in the building and the reconstruction, makes this bridge very picturesque. Most of the four arches on the left, and some of the piers were destroyed at the end of the Second World War.

CHURCH OF SANTO STEFANO
(PIAZZA SANTO STEFANO)

A tradition exists in Verona that this church, a masterpiece of Veronese Romanesque architecture, was intended to be the city's first Cathedral. An oratory existed on the site as early as the 6th cent., but it was destroyed by Theodoric and rebuilt in the 8th cent. The present building, however, was founded in the 12th cent. and the apse is the result of 14th cent. alterations. The traditional stone and brick decoration on the façade, together with the stone pillars and the hanging porch above the entrance give the church a very fine appearance. An unusual aspect of the exterior is the robust octagonal drum above the crossing.

THE INTERIOR

Typical basilica design with a central nave divided from the aisles

The church of Santo Stefano.

by powerful piers, and a raised presbytery section.

THE RIGHT SIDE

The Chapel of the Innocents (1619-1621) is decorated in exotic Baroque style with frescoes by Ottino depicting *The Assumption* and *the Virtues*. *The Massacre of the Innocents* above the altar is also by Ottino. To the right is an important work by the most famous of all Veronese 17th cent. painters, Marcantonio Bassetti, showing the *Five Bishops of Verona*, to whom the chapel is dedicated. Facing it is the *Forty Martyrs* by Orbetto. In the lunette above the side door the fresco with *Saint Stephen and the Holy Innocents* is by B. Dal Moro.

THE PRESBITERY

This is the most important part of the church, and its outstanding feature is a rare *semicircular gallery*, the columns which support it bearing capitals from the original 8th cent. church. There is also a contemporary *Bishop's Throne* (or "Cathedra"), which gave rise to the legend of this church's Cathedral status. The cupola is decorated with frescoes by Domenico Brusasorci (1523), and on the right side of the Presbytery is *The Madonna with Saints Peter and Paul* by Fr. Caroto. The left hand chapel contains the frescoed *Annunciation* and *The Coronation of the Virgin Mary*, attributed to the School of Stefano da Verona.

The church of San Giorgio in Braida.

Strikingly reminiscent of the gallery in the Presbytery. Several elements of the early building survive here, particularly the ancient *capitals* on the columns, and fragments of 13th cent. frescoes, whereas the statue of *St. Peter* is 14th cent.

CHURCH OF SAN GIORGIO IN BRAIDA

This church was founded in 1447 and designed by Antonio Ricci. It was built on the site of a small 8th cent. church, dedicated to the same saint. Around the middle of the 16th cent. the drum and the cupola were designed by Sanmicheli. He was also responsible for the belltower, which was never finished.

The facade is 17th cent. French shot spattered the house next door in 1805. The damage is still visible.

THE INTERIOR

The church, as well as being one of the richest in works of art in Verona, is also outstanding for the excellence of its design. It has one central nave, with side chapels opening off it. On the wall above the main door The *Baptism of Christ,* by Jacopo Tintoretto. At the beginning of the nave two remarkable 16th cent. *holy water stoups,* with statues of *St. John the Baptist* and *St George.*

First chapel on the right. *Christ and Mary Magdalen* by Fr. Montemezzano 16th cent. Second chapel on the right. *The Assumption of the Virgin Mary* by P. Ottino. Third chapel on the right. **Pentecost** by Domenico Tintoretto Fourth chapel on the right. *The Virgin Mary and Archangels,* an outstanding work by Domenico Brusasorci.

At each side of the Choir the two sections of a painting by Romanino, *The Judgement of St. George* (16th cent).

THE PRESBITERY

On the balustrade are *statues of the Apostles* in bronze, stylistically similar to those on the holy water stoups. To one side of the Presbytery is *The Announcing Angel,* and this is balanced on the other side by *The Virgin Mary,* both by Fr. Caroto. Behind the altar hangs one of the finest works by Paolo Veronese: *The Martyrdom of Saint George,* painted between 1565 and 1566. On each side of the 16th cent. organ is another work by Romanino in two parts - *The Martyrdom of Saint George.* Fourth chapel on the left, one of the major works of Girolamo dai Libri, *Madonna with Saints Zeno and Lorenzo Giustiniani, with Angelic Musicians.* Third chapel on the left, a *Triptych,* which includes *The Transfiguration* by Francesco Caroto; the lunette is by

Domenico Brusasorci. Second chapel on the left, *Martyrdom of Saint Laurence* by Sigism. De Stefani (1564). First chapel on the left, *Saint Ursula and the Virgins* by F. Caroto.

SANCTUARY OF THE MADONNA OF LOURDES

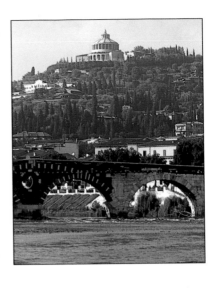

The Sanctuary of the Madonna of Lourdes rises to dominate Verona from the San Leonardo hill which encircles the Valdonega valley: the edifice sprang up in its two present forms starting in 1958 owing to events that make it one of the most significant places in the contemporary ecclesiastical history of the whole city.

According to popular tradition, the whole zone of the Valdonega was dedicated by the Crusaders, on their return from the Holy Land, to the construction of a series of oratories, because of the resemblance of some of its landscapes with places in Palestine. Thus, one church was dedicated to St Mary of Nazareth, a second one to St Mary in Bethlehem, and a third one was called Holy Cross, in reference to the hill of Calvary at Jerusalem.

On the San Leonardo hill, instead, from at least 1265 there rose a church dedicated to the Saint that had an adjoining monastery, the complex of which was to grow

The Sanctuary of the Madonna of Lourdes, on the San Leonardo hill, seen from the river Adige.
Facing page, top to bottom: *façade of the Sanctuary* and *statue of the Madonna of Lourdes.*

enormously before the dreadful earthquake that struck Verona in 1511. Today, only the Romanesque bell-tower, a part of the cloister and the apse of the church remain. In 1785, however, the monastery was de-consecrated until, thanks to its strategic position, the hill was designated by the Grand Duke, Maximilian of Hapsburg, as the seat of a military fortress, that was realised in 1838. Finally after the war, the complex, that had been used as a political prison between 1943 and 1945, was assigned to the Fathers of the Stigmatas for them to make it their new sanctuary.

Having reached Verona shortly after their foundation (1853), the

Fathers had first settled in Piazza Cittadella in what was called the Church of the Stigmatas; subsequently, owing to an increase in the religious family, they went to the church of St. Theresa which was reconsecrated to the Madonna of Lourdes and for which the sculptor Ugo Zannoni sculpted (1908) a *statue of the Virgin*, which was placed in a special

grotto. During the Allied bombing of Verona in 1945, the Church of the Stigmatas was destroyed, but the statue of the Madonna remained miraculously undamaged. In search of a new seat, the monks were assigned the old fortress of the San Leonardo hill: building of the present Sanctuary was begun in 1958 to the design of architect Paolo Rossi, over the structures of the ancient fort and with the adoption of a large body with a circular plan and protruding wings, realised with the most modern technologies involving the use of concrete. The *statue of the Madonna* was lodged in a modern new grotto on a terrace, so as to create in this way two places for worship: the actual church and the space outside the grotto open over the city.

LAKE GARDA

Lake Garda is situated only a few kilometres from Verona. This lake, originally known as Benaco, was much loved by Virgil, Catullus and

Goethe. The lake, whose waters are famed for their transparency, is considered a kind of extension of the city of Verona. Indeed, the Veronese themselves have always thought of is as "their" lake, in spite of the fact that nowadays, during the holiday season from May to September, its banks attract tourists from all over the world. The lake has many attractions for tourists: a mild climate, beautiful and varied scenery, ranging from the rolling hills at the southern end to "fiords" at the northern end. However, these natural advantages are not the only ones as further man-made attractions are being constantly developed. There are a number of amusement parks and sporting grounds which have been opened recently, and during the winter season there is plenty of good skiing on the spacious snowfields of Monte Baldo. All this makes Lake Garda one of the major attractions for visitors to Italy. Natural beauty and the picturesqueness of the ancient fishing villages around the lake have had to adapt themselves in some cases to the needs of mass tourism. However, it is to be hoped that Lake Garda will continue to offer its splendid and unique attractions throughout future years, as it does at present. Among the small towns which dot the shores of the lake are the following: Peschiera, Bardolino, Garda, San Vigilio, Torri, Castelletto, Malcesine, all under the jurisdiction of Verona; Torbole, Riva, Limone, under the jurisdiction of Trent Gargnano; Maderno, Gardone, Riviera, Salò, Desenzano, Sirmione, all of which come under Brescia.

View of Sirmione.

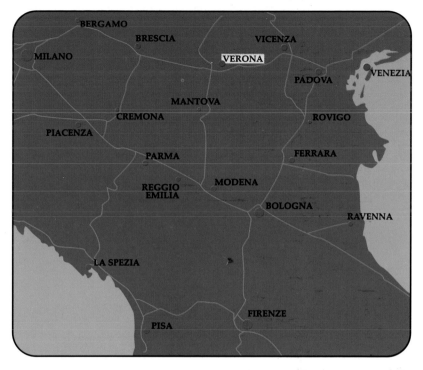

DISTANCES IN KM FROM THE PRINCIPAL ITALIAN CITIES

	Bari	Bologna	Florence	Genoa	Milan	Naples	Rome	Turin	Venice
Verona	810	140	210	290	160	715	505	290	115

TOURIST INFORMATION OFFICE

APT - P.zza Erbe, 38 ☎ 800.6997
IAT - Via Leoncino, 61 ☎ 592.828
IAT - Stazione Porta Nuova ☎ 800.0861
IAT - Via del Lavoro (fair grounds) ☎ 502.265 (seasonal openings)
CAV (cooperative of Verona hotelkeepers) ☎ 800.9844

INFORMATION

**PUBLIC
TRANSPORTATION:**
piazzale Roma
☎ 5287886

TRAINS:
Stazione Verona Porta Nuova
☎ (147) 888.088

AIRLINES:
Airport Valerio Catullo
☎ (045) 809.5666
reservations ☎ 594.222/464
Air Terminal Railroad Station
Verona
☎ (045) 800.4129
TAXIS:
Radio Taxi
☎ (045) 532.666
Radio Taxi Airport
☎ (045) 861.9222
Continuous Service
piazza Bra
☎ (045) 803.0565
Porta Nuova Station
☎ (045) 800.4528
Daytime Service
piazza Erbe
☎ (045) 803.0561
Borgo Trento Hospital
☎ (045) 834.9511
Porta San Giorgio
☎ (045) 834.9510

PARKING:
Parking Arena
via Bentegodi
☎ (045) 800.9333
Garage Italia
corso Porta Nuova, 91
☎ (045) 800.6312

Parking Cittadella
p.zza Cittadella, 4
☎ (045) 595.593
Nuova Borsa - via Locatelli, 6

**POST AND TELEGRAPH
OFFICE**
Informazioni ☎ 800.3998
Telegrammi ☎ 186

EMERGENCY PHONE NUMBERS

☎

Police Emergency.	.113
Police:	
municipal......................	**807.8411**
highway...........................	**500.333**
Carabinieri:	
Emergency aid.......................	**112**
Fire brigade...........................	**115**
First Aid Services:	
Verona Emergency...........	**582.222**
Ambulances:	
Croce Bianca...................	**803.3700**
Croce Verde...................	**800.1111**
Hospitals:	
Civile Maggiore	
(BorgoTrento).................	**807.1111**
Policlinico (Borgo Roma)	**807.1111**
Doctor on call:	
Verona Centro.................	**807.5627**
Verona Sud....................	**580.222**
Verona Est....................	**892.1500**
City Hall:	
switchboard....................	**809.0611**
foreigners division..........	**809.0505**
ACI..................................	**595.333**
Lost and Found	
ATM (city buses).............	**8005825**
Railways.	**809.3827**
Vigili Urbani....................	**807.8411**

MONEY EXCHANGE

Cassa di Risparmio
via Cappello, 1 - piazza Brà, 26/a - viale del Lavoro (Fair-Agricenter)
Banca Popolare di Verona
corso Porta Nuova, 4 - Aeroporto V. Catullo - via Mazzini, 30/b
Credito Italiano
via Mazzini, 41/a
Banca Popolare di Bergamo
piazza Brà, 4
Exchange Office Porta Nuova RR. Station
(open every day 7 am to 9 pm)

Many banking agencies in the historical center have automatic tellers for exchange.

MUSEUMS•MONUMENTS•LIBRARIES

Arena Amphitheatre   ☎ 800.3204
piazza Brà • closed Mondays
open: 8am-7pm / opera season 8am-3pm
Arche Scaligere
via Arche Scaligere • visible externally
Juliet's House   ☎ 803.4303
via Cappello, 23 • closed Mondays
open: 8am-7pm
Roman Theatre and Archaeological Museum   ☎ 800.0360
Regaste Redentore, 2 • closed Mondays
open: 8am-1pm
Juliet's Tomb and the Fresco Museum   ☎ 800.0361
via del Pontiere, 5 • closed Mondays
open: 8am-7pm
Lamberti Tower   ☎ 803.2726
p.zza Signori, courtyard Merc. Vecchio
closed Mondays - open: 9am-7pm
Giusti Gardens   ☎ 803.4029
via Giardino Giusti, 2 • open every day
open: winter 9am-sunset / summer 9am-8pm
African Museum   ☎ 800.2418
vic. Pozzo, 1 (S. Giovanni in Valle) • closed Mondays
open: weekdays 9-12am/3-6pm / holidays 3-7pm
Museo di Castelvecchio   ☎ 594.734
corso Castelvecchio, 2 • closed Mondays
open: 8am-7pm

Natural History Museum ☎ 807.9400
lgd. Porta Vittoria, 9 · closed Fridays
open: Mon-Sat 8am-7pm / Sunday 1:30-7pm

Museo Lapidario Maffeiano ☎ 590.087
piazza Brà, 28 · closed Mondays open: 8am-1pm

Gallery of Modern Art 'Palazzo Forti' ☎ 800.1903
entrance Corso S. Anastasia - closed Mondays
open: 9am-7pm / summer exhibits 9am-10pm

Fondazione Museo Miniscalchi Erizzo ☎ 803.2484
via S. Mamaso, 2/A · closed Mondays
open: Tues-Sat 1-7pm / Sun 10:30-12:30/4-7pm

Railroad Museum ☎ 809.2412
Magazzino Centrale Logistico, Verona P.ta Vescovo,
Porto S. Pancrazio
previous reservations required

Museo delle Carrozze dell'800 'Cav. G. Giorgi' ☎ 829.8111
at the Agricenter, Verona Fair
open during the Fieragricola and the Fieracavalli

Chapter Library - Canonic Museum ☎ 596.516
p.zza Duomo, 13 · closed Thurs. and Sun. - closed July
open: 9:30-12:30 / Tues. and Fri 9:30-12:30/4-6pm

Municipal Library ☎ 807.9710
via Cappello, 43 · closed holidays open: 8:30 am - 6:30 pm
sat. and July-August 8:30am-1:30pm

FAIRS   open 8am-2pm

Tuesdays
·piazza San Zeno
·via U. Maddalena (Saval)
·via Avogadro (San Massimo)
·via Plinio (B.go Venezia)
·piazza Isolo

Wednesdays
·viale Commercio (B.go Roma)
·p.zza S.ta Toscana (P.ta Vescovo)
·largo Marzabotto (B.go Trento)
·via Poerio (Ponte Crencano)
·piazza Brodolini (Golosine)

Thursdays
·via Prina (Golosine)
·via Villafranca (Santa Lucia)
·via Monte Bianco (S. Michele)
·Parona

Fridays
·piazza S. Zeno
·piazza S.ta Toscana
·p.zza degli Arditi (Volto S. Luca)
·via Maddalena (Saval)
·Montorio

Saturdays
·piazzale Olimpia (Stadium)

* Craft, Art, Antique Fair in S. Zeno the 3rd Saturday of every month

CINEMAS·THEATRES

Ariston
via XX Settembre, 119
☎ 596.035

Astra
via Oberdan, 13
☎ 596.327

Corallo
via 4 Spade, 19
☎ 595.990

Ciak
via XX Settembre, 100
☎ 803.0972

Filarmonico
via Roma, 3
☎ 596.826

Fiume
vicolo Cere
☎ 800.2050

Marconi
via Mazzini, 15
☎ 594.708

Nuovo
p.zza Viviani, 10
☎ 800.6100

Odeon
via S. Antonio, 19
☎ 800.3272

Pindemonte
via Sabotino, 2/b
☎ 913.591

Rivoli
p.zza Brà
☎ 590.855

Teatro Alcione
via Verdi, 20
☎ 840.0848

DISCOTHEQUES

Alter Ego, via Torcelle, 9
☎ 915.130-834.3016
Wen./Fri./Sat.

Berfi's Club, via Lussemburgo, 1
☎ 508.024
Wen./Thurs./Fri./Sat./Sun.

Dorian Gray, via Belobono, 13

☎ 540.206
Fri./Sat.

Grace, via Provolo, 24
☎ 597.858
Wen./Fri./Sat.

Queen, via Bertoni, 1
☎ 801.3463-592.500
Wen./Fri./Sat.

PIANO BAR

Boomerang, vicolo Guasto, 15
☎ 800.9811

Bar Emanuel, p.zza Brà, 6
☎ 590.154

Caffè Dante, p.zza dei Signori
☎ 595.249

Caffè delle Erbe, p.zza Erbe, 32
☎ 591.403

Caffè Orchidea, p.zza Erbe, 20
☎ 591.512

Caffè Filippini, p.zza Erbe, 26
☎ 800.4549

HOTELS

*****

Gabbia d'Oro, corso Porta Borsari, 4/A   ☎ 800.3060

****

Accademia, via Scala, 12	☎	596.222
Colomba d'Oro, via C. Cattaneo, 10	☎	595.300
Due Torri Hotel Baglioni, piazza S. Anastasia, 4	☎	595.044
Euromotel Croce Bianca, via Bresciana, 2	☎	890.3890
Firenze, corso Porta Nuova, 88	☎	801.1510
Forte Agip, via Unità d'Italia, 346	☎	972.033
Grand Hotel, corso Porta Nuova, 105	☎	595.600
Ibis, via E. Fermi, 11/C	☎	820.3720
Leopardi, via G. Leopardi, 16	☎	810.1444
Montresor Hotel Giberti, via Giberti, 7	☎	800.6900
Montresor Hotel Palace, via Galvani, 19	☎	575.700
San Luca, vic. Volto S. Luca, 8	☎	591.333
San Marco, via Longhena, 42	☎	569.011
Victoria, via Adua, 8	☎	590.566

***

Antica Porta Leona, corticella Leoni, 3	☎	595.499
Bologna, p.tta Scalette Rubiani, 3	☎	800.6830
Borghetti, p.tta Valpolicella, 47	☎	942.366
Brandoli, via Antonio da Legnago, 11	☎	884.0155
Corte Ongaro Residence, via Scuderlando, 40	☎	820.4260
De' Capuleti, via del Pontiere, 26	☎	800.0154
Elefante, via Bresciana, 27	☎	890.3700
Europa, via Roma, 8	☎	800.2882
Gardenia, via Unità d'Italia, 350	☎	972.122
Giulietta e Romeo, vicolo Tre Marchetti, 3	☎	800.3554
Italia, via G. Mameli, 58/66	☎	918.088
Martini, via G. Camuzzoni, 2	☎	569.128
Mastino, corso Porta Nuova, 16	☎	595.388
Maxim, via Belviglieri, 42	☎	840.1800
Milano, vicolo Tre Marchetti, 11	☎	596.011
Mini Hotel Brennero, via Brennero, 3	☎	941.100
Monaco, via Torricelli, 4	☎	580.809
Montresor Hotel S. Pietro, via S. Teresa, 1	☎	582.600
Novo Hotel Rossi, via delle Coste, 2	☎	569.022
Piccolo Hotel, via G. Camuzzoni, 3/B	☎	569.400
Porta Palio, via Col. Galliano, 21	☎	810.2140

HOTELS

Sud Point Hotel, via E. Fermi, 13/B   ☎ 820.0922
Touring, via Quintino Sella, 15   ☎ 590.944
Verona, corso Porta Nuova, 47/49   ☎ 594.341

**

Al Cigno, corso Milano, 26   ☎ 565.156
Aurora, piazzetta XIV Novembre, 2   ☎ 594.717
Elena, via Mastino della Scala, 9   ☎ 820.0920
Garda, via Gardesana, 35   ☎ 890.3877
Gardenia (annex), via Unità d'Italia, 350   ☎ 972.122
Mazzanti, via Mazzanti, 6   ☎ 800.6813
Sanmicheli, via Valverde, 2   ☎ 800.3749
Scalzi, via Carmelitani Scalzi, 5   ☎ 590.422
Selene (hotel tourist res.), via Bresciana, 81   ☎ 851.0318
Serenissima, viale del Lavoro, 24   ☎ 501.858
Siena, via Marconi, 41   ☎ 800.3074
Siros, via Bengasi, 26/A   ☎ 820.4130
Torcolo, vicolo Listone, 3   ☎ 800.7512
Trento, corso Porta Nuova, 36   ☎ 596.444
Trieste, corso Porta Nuova, 57   ☎ 596.022
Valverde, via Valverde, 91   ☎ 803.3611

*

Al Castello, corso Cavour, 43   ☎ 800.4403
Alla Cancellata, via Col. Fincato 4/6   ☎ 532.820
Alla Grotta, via Bresciana, 16   ☎ 890.3865
Arena, stradone Porta Palio, 2   ☎ 803.2440
Armando, via Dietro Pallone, 1   ☎ 800.0206
Catullo and annex, via Valerio Catullo, 1   ☎ 800.2786
Cavour, vicolo Chiodo, 4/B   ☎ 590.166
Ciopeta, vicolo Teatro Filarmonico, 2   ☎ 800.6843
Da Romano, via Tombetta, 39   ☎ 505.228
Gelmini, via Belfiore, 54   ☎ 540.240

HOSTELS
Ostello della Gioventù, salita Fontana di Ferro, 15   ☎ 590.0360

CAMP SITES
Giulietta e Romeo, strada Bresciana, 54 (Ca' dell'Ebreo)   ☎ 851.0243
Castel San Pietro, via Castel S. Pietro, 2   ☎ 592.037

RESTAURANTS

12 Apostoli, vicolo Corticella San Marco, 3 ☎ 596.999
Accademia, via Scala, 10 ☎ 806.6072
Al Castello, corso Cavour, 43 ☎ 800.4403
All'Aquila- Due Torri, p.zza S. Anastasia, 4 ☎ 595.044
Alla Torre, p.zza Erbe, 8-10 ☎ 803.1230
Antica Trattoria da l'Almelia, lgd. B. Rubele, 32 ☎ 800.5526
Antico Caffè Dante, p.zza dei Signori ☎ 800.3593
Arche, via Arche Scaligere, 6 ☎ 800.7415
Arcovolo, via Leoncino, 29 ☎ 803.1212
Bologna, p.tta Scalette Rubiani, 3 ☎ 800.6830
Bottega del Vino, via Scudo di Francia, 3 ☎ 800.4535
Cesare Sottoriva, via Sottoriva, 42 ☎ 800.2255
Ciopeta, vicolo Teatro Filarmonico, 2 ☎ 800.6843
El Cantinon, via San Rocchetto, 11 ☎ 595.291
El Mocoleto, via Stella, 13 ☎ 803.0066
Greppia, vicolo Samaritana, 3 ☎ 800.4577
Il Cenacolo, via Teatro Filarmonico, 10 ☎ 592.288
Il Desco, dietro S. Sebastiano, 7 ☎ 595.358
La Pigna, via Pigna, 4/b ☎ 800.4080
Maffei, p.zza Erbe, 38 ☎ 801.0015
Mazzanti, via Mazzanti, 6 ☎ 801.0855
Millevoglie, via Marconi, 72 ☎ 597.517
Nuovo Marconi, via dalle Fogge, 4 ☎ 591.910
Osteria Sgarzarie, corte Sgarzarie ☎ 800.0312
S. Eufemia, via Francesco Emilei, 21/b ☎ 800.6865
Scaligero, via Amatore Sciesa, 27 ☎ 803.0001
Torcolo, via C. Cattaneo, 11 ☎ 803.0440
Tre Risotti, via Poloni, 15 ☎ 594.408
Veronantica, via Sottoriva, 10/a ☎ 800.4124

RESTAURANTS • PIZZERIE

Al Bracere, via Adigetto, 6/a ☎ 597.062
Al Dollaro, corso Porta Nuova, 78 ☎ 803.2341
Alla Costa, via della Costa, 2 ☎ 597.468
Cantore, via A. Mario, 2 ☎ 803.1830
Delle Nazioni, via Oriani, 2 ☎ 803.3503
Du de Cope, Galleria Pellicciai, 10 ☎ 595.562
Il Calice, via Pallone, ☎ 800.4892
Impero, p.zza dei Signori, 8 ☎ 803.0160
Liston, via Dietro Liston, 19 ☎ 803.4003

RESTAURANTS·PIZZERIE

Marechiaro, via S. Antonio, 15/a ☎ 800.4506
Nastro Azzurro, vicolo Listone, 4 ☎ 800.4457
Olivo, p.zza Brà, 18 ☎ 803.0598
Pallone, via del Pontiere, 3 ☎ 801.1530
Pam Pam, corso P.ta Borsari, 55 ☎ 803.0363
Quo Vadis S.r.l., via Leoni, 13 ☎ 800.2224

TRATTORIE

Al Bersagliere, via Dietro Pallone, 1 ☎ 800.4824
Al Pompiere, viale Regina d'Ungheria, 5 ☎ 803.0537
Alla Colonna, largo Pescheria Vecchia, 4 ☎ 596.718
Alla Pergola, p.tta S. M. in Solaro, 10 ☎ 800.4744
Bar Turco, p.zza Erbe, 14 ☎ 800.4504
Boomerang, vicolo del Guasto, 15 ☎ 594.157
Dal Ropeton, via S. Giovanni in Valle, 46 ☎ 803.0040
F.lli Orlandi, c.so Porta Nuova, 115/a ☎ 581.344
La Fontanina, via Trota, 11 ☎ 803.1133
Osteria al Carro Armato, vicolo Gatto, 2/a ☎ 803.0175
Osteria al Duca, via Arche Scaligere, 2 ☎ 594.474
Osteria Sgarzerie, via Corte Sgarzerie, 14/a ☎ 800.0312
S. Anastasia, c.so S. Anastasia, 27 ☎ 800.9177
Scalin, via Marconi, 28 ☎ 800.4520
Tre Marchetti, vicolo Tre Marchetti ☎ 803.0463

PIZZERIE

Da 'Salvatore', c.so Porta Borsari, 39 ☎ 803.0366
Ponte Navi, via Dogani, 1/a ☎ 591.203
Vesuvio 3, corso S. Anastasia, 20 ☎ 595.460

SELF-SERVICE

Fast-food Alfredo Alfredo, via Mazzini, 75 ☎ 801.1644
Brek, p.zza Brà, 20 ☎ 800.4561
Tavola Calda G&G, via Fama, 6/b ☎ 800.9660
Mc Donald's, corso Porta Nuova, 14 ☎ 597.422
Melody, via Roma, 13/vicolo Ghiaia, 7 ☎ 800.2053
Taverna degli Scaligeri, via Sottoriva, 24 ☎ 590.302
S. Matteo, via del Guasto, 5

INDEX